Diversity Primer

Diversity Best Practices

BONNIER
Corporation

Diversity Primer

Published by:

Diversity Best Practices
2 Park Avenue
New York, NY 10016
212.219.7470
DiversityBestPractices.com

For additional copies, contact Diversity Best Practices at 212.219.7470
or visit www.diversitybestpractices.com

ISBN: 978-0-9833060-0-9

Printed in the United States of America

Diversity encompasses the many dimensions that make us who we are as individuals. It includes all of the differences that make us unique, including but not limited to race, ethnicity, language, nationality, sexual orientation, religion, gender, socioeconomic status, age, and physical and mental ability. As human beings, we are much more similar than we are different. However, our differences matter.

Diversity adds complexity to the workplace and when combined with strategies to promote and sustain an inclusive workplace environment, it becomes a competitive advantage and bottom-line contributor.

Organizations succeed and thrive by maximizing the potential of a diverse workforce to gain full benefit of an ever-expanding global economy. Simply having a diverse workforce is not enough to create institutional change. For organizations to succeed and thrive, they must create environments that support and actively enable mutual respect and opportunities to maximize individual potential.

We are challenged every day to understand the impact of our own cultural viewpoints on our interactions with others. Both internal and external barriers can impede respect and relationship-building with others who are different. Through education, training, self-reflection, and exposure to different cultures, we can expand our world view and reduce these internal and external barriers. This lifelong learning process, known as cultural competence, results in new knowledge, skills, behaviors, and attitudes; enhances our ability to work effectively with others from different cultural backgrounds; and increases an organization's ability to maximize the benefits of diversity within their workforces.

Indeed, the financial benefits of diversity to corporations are as great as the social ones in today's evolving marketplace. Today there are opportunities to market to different groups like never before, and all stakeholders—from shareholders to vendors to customers to employees—are seeing that advancing diversity and inclusion is a "must-do" that makes money.

The business leaders profiled in this primer reveal their commitment to diversity and inclusion as a way to be innovative and competitive. They take advantage of every opportunity with the idea to create a new business culture that is progressive, inclusive—and lucrative.

Contents

Chapter 1 | # Diversity & Inclusion: An Overview

Contributor: National MultiCultural Institute

In corporate America, a common mission, vision, and purpose in thought and action across all levels of an organization is of the utmost importance to bottom line success, but at the same time, so is the celebration, validation, and respect of each individual and the unique attributes he or she brings to the table. Effectively combining these two fundamental areas requires diligence, understanding, and trust from all parties, and one way organizations are attempting to bridge the gap is through diversity and inclusion initiatives. But before an organization can make true progress in this regard, people across all levels of the organization must understand and believe in the company's definitions of diversity and inclusion.

Diversity and inclusion is not a buzz word but a business imperative tied directly to the business case of the best companies in America and around the globe. In best practice companies, diversity and inclusion is not only viewed as an asset to the organization and employees, it is a necessity. As corporations look to build their bottom lines through increased employee engagement, robust recruitment and retention initiatives, and insightful marketing plans, diversity and inclusion will continue to rise to the fore as essential for growth and achievement.

In this chapter, we explore the following questions:

- What are the four stages of diversity and inclusion, and where is your organization on the continuum?

- What are some corporate definitions of diversity and inclusion?

Diversity & Inclusion Structure

The diversity and inclusion (D&I) field has experienced exponential growth over the past decade. Fueled by tremendous demographic, economic, political and social realities, and marketplace demand, more and more organizations are recognizing that their future success is inextricably tied to their ability to tap into this new workforce and customer base.

While most companies today recognize the critical importance of diversity and inclusion to their competitiveness, there are various stages of evolution to diversity and inclusion work. Therefore, it is important to understand the history of D&I work in the United States, in order to articulate what D&I and cultural competence mean in the present day and in the future for organizational success.

Continuum of Organizational Diversity Work

Civil Rights	Affirmative Action	Managing Diversity and Inclusion	Diversity and Inclusion as a Strategic Imperative

The stages of diversity and inclusion work within organizations often reflect this continuum, from a focus on legal requirements and compliance to fully embedding diversity and inclusion within core business strategies and practices.

Civil Rights

The Civil Rights era focused on formally addressing the historic discrimination that had legally denied minorities full rights of citizenship. Laws were designed to ensure equal treatment to women and racial minorities by protecting people from discrimination in education, employment, housing, and other opportunities based on race, color, national origin, religion, or gender. The laws, primarily Title VII of the Civil Rights Act of 1964, the Equal Pay Act of 1963, and the Age Discrimination in Employment Act of 1967, were created to level the playing field for all. Additional laws were enacted in subsequent years to expand civil rights protections—Sections 501 and 505 of the Rehabilitation Act of 1973, Title I and Title V of the American Disabilities Act of 1990, and the Civil Rights Act of 1991.

Affirmative Action

Affirmative Action began in the 1970s as a strategy to recruit and hire a more diverse workforce. Focused primarily on representation, Affirmative Action policies were intended to address past discrimination by giving preferential treatment to specified underrepresented groups in the workplace. The objective was to make the employer's workforce more representative of the general population in its geographic area. There are strong opinions both for and against Affirmative Action. Those against Affirmative Action often argue that such policies result in reverse discrimination and in hiring unqualified and under qualified candidates. Proponents, on the other hand, often argue diverse candidates will not have equal access to opportunities unless organizations mandate their recruitment.

Whatever one's opinion about Affirmative Action, organizations at this stage on the D&I continuum will have only limited success in efforts to gain competitive advantage through a more diverse workforce. A more diverse employee base does not automatically provide an environment where individual employees are encouraged to contribute their full talents toward organizational success nor does it ensure that diversity and inclusion will be represented at all levels of the organization. To move beyond a focus on representation, Affirmative Action strategies will need to be supported by conscious efforts to create inclusive environments where diverse perspectives are heard and acted on.

The Four Stages of Diversity & Inclusion

The first step in growing your company's commitment to diversity & inclusion (D&I) is to assess where it now stands. Most diversity & inclusion strategies in corporate America reside in one of four common stages of evolution, from working to meet EEO and legal requirements to integrating diversity philosophy into the business mission of the company.

What stage best defines your organization?

Stage I: EEO and Legal Compliance

Diversity & inclusion initiatives, once unheard of in corporate America, have come a long way to become a central part of the critical business function. The early corporate emphasis was on equal employment, legal mandates, and reporting to the Equal Employment Opportunity Commission (EEOC).

Original diversity initiatives were reactive because they aimed to prevent discrimination and litigation. Today's diversity & inclusion initiatives must be proactive and viewed as a business imperative by company leadership—a core function that fuels a company's competitive edge.

Stage II: Affirmative Action and Hiring of First Diversity Officers

In this stage, Affirmative Action becomes a serious goal. Companies begin to name diversity officers and spend money on scholarships and community activities to support a growing minority workforce. For these companies, such diversity & inclusion initiatives follow closely with community relations and corporate philanthropy, yet only under Stage IV do we witness a sophisticated approach to community and philanthropy.

Stage III: Targeted D&I Recruitment and Retention

In stage three, diversity & inclusion becomes a recruitment and retention tool, helping human resources seek out the best and brightest employees from all backgrounds. Companies tout diversity and inclusion as a workforce imperative, building their companies as microcosms of an ever-diversifying world. For many, this emphasis proves vital to match the workforce changes with those of the marketplace.

Stage IV: Integrating D&I Into the Corporate Business Model

Functional integration with recruitment, retention, and work/life, along with the other key functions—such as customer and marketplace, community outreach, corporate philanthropy, government relations, marketing, and supplier diversity—allow companies and organizations to make diversity & inclusion central to their brand, business practices, and culture. Diversity and inclusion is managed in a far more strategic way, typically including the measurement of the entire process and of specific D&I components. In this stage, the CEO and Board of Directors lend support and endorsement, of which the most important is the recognition that diversity and inclusion increases revenue while decreasing costs and is a competitive advantage. Diversity and inclusion is a management imperative of company leadership and well-articulated in every aspect of the organization and companies establish employee resource groups to unite different groups of employees and diversity councils to help guide the company's diversity and inclusion efforts

Managing Diversity and Inclusion

Due in part to the gains of Affirmative Action, organizations increased the diversity of their workforce; however, this success revealed the natural tension and challenges that often accompany such change. Two phenomena often accompanied the more representative workplace environment: The "revolving door" syndrome, with newly recruited underrepresented employees not staying with their employers very long; and second, people neither working well together, nor trusting each other across cultural lines.

To address the problems that accompanied the new workplace, organizations began to offer D&I training with the expectation that if employees could better understand, become more aware, and more sensitive to others, they could get along better. Such training yielded limited success but led to the concept of Managing Diversity, a main goal of which is to enable and tap into the potential of all employees. Organizations began to develop and implement strategies for organizational change—change that would produce a more inclusive culture. This concept was a multifaceted approach that addressed both individual and organizational responsibilities for building inclusive environments. New systems, procedures, and training to enhance, support, and encourage opportunities for previously underrepresented groups were recognized as essential to organizational success. It is also in this stage that the Chief Diversity Officer role began to be recognized as a major value-add for organizational success.

Diversity and Inclusion as Strategic Imperative

Organizations that recognize that diversity and inclusion is critical to their long-term business success have begun to adopt strategic initiatives that are aligned with and central to overall organizational goals. Chief Diversity Officers often have a seat at the strategy table, holding individual managers and senior leaders accountable for achieving diversity and inclusion objectives. These organizations are at the forefront of developing best practices and are using a growing body of research on topics, ranging from the efficacy of diversity and inclusion training to implicit bias to micro-messaging, to inform their business practices.

Questions for Reflection:

1. How deep is your knowledge/involvement in the evolution of diversity and inclusion work?

2. How has your organization historically addressed diversity and inclusion throughout the decades?

3. Where do you want the organization to be in 2020, 2050, and beyond?

4. What policies/practices currently exist at your organization to support diversity and inclusion?

5. What steps can you take to help your organization move forward on the diversity and inclusion continuum?

Conclusion

In this chapter, we:

• Discussed the four stages of diversity and inclusion in terms of a continuum.

• Shared corporate definitions of diversity and inclusion.

When taken as an interrelated whole, diversity, inclusion, and cultural competence allow organizations to truly leverage the rich skills and experiences of their employees and deliver products and services that are uniquely tailored to the needs and wants of their customers. Companies that seek to excel in the coming years and secure their place as global leaders must make diversity and inclusion a strategic imperative.

Diversity can add complexity to the workplace, but when that diversity is nurtured through cultural competence to create an environment of inclusion, it becomes a competitive advantage and bottom line contributor.

Corporate Examples: Diversity Website Statements

Abbott Laboratories

Simply defined, diversity recognizes similarities and differences. Inclusion builds a foundation where employees can reach their full potential by embracing concepts such as awareness, acceptance, respect and understanding. Our goal is to create an inclusive culture at Abbott that enables all employees to contribute to our company's success and to develop their talents, strengths, and careers. Diversity and Inclusion are more than just beliefs; they are priorities. With approximately 70,000 employees in more than 130 countries, we place a premium on having a high–performing employee population that reflects the customers and markets we serve.

Dell

At Dell we characterize Global Diversity by similarities and differences, defining it more broadly than just race, gender and ethnicity. It's about diversity of thinking, leadership, skill set and style. And by harnessing our differences in pursuit of common business goals, our teams can bring about innovation and new ways of achieving objectives. Diversity represents a way of doing business that is barrier-free and all-inclusive, allowing the unique ideas, experiences, cultures and backgrounds of all our people to come together for creating the most innovative products and best customer experience. Our diversity is global in its inclusion and respect for the many different people and cultures we encounter everyday throughout the many countries in which we do business worldwide.

Eastman Kodak Company

Diversity at Eastman Kodak Company refers to the degree and depth of richness represented by the population of people supporting Kodak, along the dimensions of civilization orientation, national identification, organizational factors, societal formation, individual identification, and personality/style. Inclusion is the search for value and full, effective utilization of the richness of Kodak's human capital. Human capital includes Kodak's board of directors, customers, employees, and external business alliances.

Exelon Corporation

Diversity at Exelon is the many distinct characteristics that employees, suppliers and customers bring to our organization. These include race/ethnicity/national origin, gender, age, sexual orientation, socio-economic background, physical abilities, religion, and other differences that create an inclusive environment. And with these distinct characteristics come variations of thinking, communications styles, skill and behaviors—all of which enable us to achieve our business goals, gain competitive advantage and support our business values.

Hewlett-Packard

Diversity is the existence of many unique individuals in the workplace, marketplace and community. This includes men and women from different nations, cultures, ethnic groups, generations, backgrounds, skills, abilities and all the other unique differences that make each of us who we are.

Inclusion means a work environment where everyone has an opportunity to fully participate in creating business success and where each person is valued for his or her distinctive skills, experiences and perspectives. Inclusion is also about creating a global community where HP connects everyone and everything through our products, services and our winning workforce.

Johnson & Johnson

Across the Johnson & Johnson Family of Companies, global diversity is defined as a variety of similar and different characteristics among people including age, gender, race, religion, national origin, physical ability, sexual orientation, thinking style, background and all other attributes that make each person unique.

Target Corporation

At Target, diversity is defined inclusively as individuality. This individuality may include a wide spectrum of attributes such as personal style, age, race, gender, ethnicity, sexual orientation, gender identity or expression, language, physical ability, religion, family, citizenship status, socioeconomic circumstances, education and life experiences. To us, diversity is any attribute that makes an individual unique that does not interfere with effective job performance.

The Coca-Cola Company

The Coca-Cola Company strives for an inclusive culture that is defined by our seven core values: leadership, passion, integrity, collaboration, innovation, quality, and accountability. Each day we work to bring these values to life through our diversity workplace strategy. This strategy includes programs to attract, retain, and develop diverse talent; provide support systems for groups with diverse backgrounds; and educate all associates so that we master the skills to achieve sustainable growth.

Coca-Cola defines diversity as: respecting individuals, valuing differences, and representing our consumers and the markets where we do business. Our diversity strategy is centered on the 4Cs: a focus on driving consumption, fostering commitment, building a culture that values diverse perspectives, and promoting effective communication and mutual understanding.

Case Study: Accenture

Since its inception, Accenture has been governed by its core values—Stewardship, Best People, Client Value Creation, One Global Network, Respect for the Individual, and Integrity—which are at the heart of everything the company does. As Accenture's business grows to develop and cultivate workforces across 49 countries, effective collaboration demands understanding the culture and character of the company.

Accenture engages its senior leadership to teach diversity's advantages when it hosts "Leading a Diverse Workforce" workshops, and the company helps its people around the world learn to work and team effectively within the organization and with clients through courses such as "Building Cross Cultural Awareness." Whether Accenture professionals are working with a small team or managing a large project involving delivery centers and outsourcing businesses across the globe, such training illustrates the value of connecting divergent styles so the company can deliver professional services in concert.

Accenture sponsors programs that encourage understanding and tolerance of race, age, gender, sexual orientation, and faith. Accenture is engaged in the recruitment, retention, and advancement of professionals who are focused on high performance.

Employee Network Groups

Accenture runs 13 network groups for employees available in each of the countries in which the company operates. Groups meet regularly, participating in talks and social visits covering diverse areas that include age, gender, sexuality, race, and faith.

Accenture Mentors Minority College Students

In 2004, Accenture piloted Commitment to Empower Successful Students, a program designed to mentor minority college students. Participants in the first-year pilot program included sophomores from Penn State, Purdue University, Stanford University, University of Michigan, and University of Texas. Students selected to participate are pursuing a technical or business major and demonstrated at least a 3.0 GPA and a clear and concise writing style.

As part of this three-year program, students shadowed Accenture employees, attended networking lunches to help establish mentoring relationships, and participated in Accenture's Student Leadership Conference the summer after their second mentoring year. Through this program, Accenture helped participants gain valuable exposure to the business world, explore the consulting career path, and understand what companies are looking for when hiring.

Accenture International Women's Day 2009

In March 2009, Accenture sponsored its fifth annual celebration of International Women's Day—a day designated by the United Nations to recognize women's contributions to the world's economy. This year, Accenture's celebration included live events for employees and clients in more than 100 locations in 29 countries, as well as an online event for Accenture's more than 186,000 employees around the world.

Accenture's theme last year, Stretch Yourself, focused on ways to manage your career and know when it's time to seek more challenging work roles. In conjunction with International Women's Day, Accenture also published original research that looks at the ways in which women around the world challenge themselves at work—and the opportunities they have to use "stretch" roles to succeed.

Training and Development

At Accenture, training and development is taken very seriously. In fact, the company even wrote a book on it. *Return on Learning*, published in 2007, tells the story of how Accenture reignited learning for a whole new generation of Accenture people, including its award-winning study demonstrating the return the company makes on its learning investment. Every employee's Accenture Education experience begins the first day he or she walks through the door and continues throughout his or her career.

New Joiner Orientation and Core Curriculum

Soon after joining Accenture, employees attend New Joiner Orientation. This multi-day class experience gives new hires the essential knowledge they need to launch their Accenture careers, whether they are straight out of university or a workforce veteran. Since New Joiner Orientation is a world-wide program, it serves as employees' introduction to Accenture's one global network. But since it is conducted near employees' homes, they also get location-specific information.

New Joiner Orientation is just the first element of the Accenture Education curriculum. The curriculum is the set of courses and learning experiences that employees complete to receive the basic, foundational knowledge they need to succeed at each level of their careers. Employees join with colleagues from all over the world, either virtually or live, to collaborate and learn together.

One Global Network... for Learning

"One Global Network" is one of Accenture's core values, and this plays out fully in the way the company's employees learn. Many Accenture people attend core training courses at the Q Center, outside of Chicago, Illinois, or at one of the regional training centers near London, England and Kuala Lumpur, Malaysia. At these locations, Accenture people from around the world gather to learn from each other, collaborate, and build professional relationships that can last for a career. Other classroom-based courses are held at regional locations around the world.

But at Accenture, learning does not stop when employees walk out of the classroom. Accenture's single global learning portal, my Learning, directs employees to over 20,000 online courses, virtual classroom courses, and other learning resources to meet almost any business need. Furthermore, Accenture offers specialized training to employees in their Consulting, Enterprise, Services, and Accenture Technology Solutions divisions.

Accenture's Commitment to Training

A recent research study shows that for every hour of training Accenture's competitors give their people, Accenture employees receive two hours, at half the cost per hour. Specifically, the company's $900 million investment in training resulted in an average of 75 training hours per person, for a total of more than 12 million hours of training delivered.

In fact, Accenture is setting the standard for learning at work. Accenture Education programs have been recognized and honored around the business world, winning prestigious awards such as the CLO Magazine Gold Award for Leading Business Change, the Most Admired Knowledge Enterprise (MAKE) award from the Knowledge Network, and multiple Brandon Hall Excellence in eLearning awards.

The Future of Learning

As excited as the company is about the Accenture Education experience, it understands there is always room to improve. Accenture continually reviews and revises its learning products, ensuring they are up-to-date with the latest ideas, information, and needs of the marketplace.

Beyond just the content, the company is recreating the way that Accenture people learn. Accenture's Center for Learning Innovation is a group of key learning leaders that is continually developing, testing, and implementing new ways for Accenture people to learn. From training on mobile devices to interactive conversations that feel more like a video game than a training course, the company's focus on innovation guarantees that Accenture people will always be on the leading edge of learning.

Case Study: Cisco Systems Inc.

Vision and Strategy

Cisco's commitment to inclusion and diversity (I&D) makes it a better company, a better global competitor, and a better corporate citizen. By fully embracing the human network in all its multiplicity, Cisco fosters innovation and talent in the workplace and engages more effectively with its customers and partners in the worldwide marketplace.

Cisco is executing on its commitment to I&D by:

- Sponsoring I&D initiatives and providing visibility at the executive level

- Forming the Global Inclusion and Diversity Council in 2007

- Building diversity into the recruiting and hiring process

- Providing mandatory manager and employee training in diversity and actively promoting a culture of inclusion

- Implementing tools and processes to develop I&D awareness, manage a diverse and often virtual workforce, and promote behavior change

- Providing supplemental development opportunities to diverse populations

Cisco formed the Global Inclusion and Diversity Council in 2007 to integrate Inclusion & Diversity (I&D) into its business processes and operations at all levels. The council is led by the Senior Vice President of Human Resources Brian Schipper and supported by sponsors at the executive level, reporting directly to Cisco's operating committee.

The role of the council includes:

- Developing the I&D vision, strategy, and execution plan

- Chartering new Employee Resource Groups; in 2008 it chartered the Cisco Disability Awareness Network, Service Member Veterans and Family Support Group, and Cisco Legacy Leaders

- Advocating policies that support an inclusive environment

- Coauthoring a new inclusion index for the Cisco Employee Satisfaction Survey

- Implementing metrics for measuring the impact of I&D initiatives

Council members also serve as executive sponsors for major diversity programs and are key communicators of the diversity message.

Another important way that Cisco cultivates I&D is through employee resource groups (ERGs). These employee-driven, company-supported affinity groups enable Cisco employees to connect with others who share a similar culture, identity, interest, or career goal. Open to employees around the world, ERGs provide social networking and professional-development support, while also offering opportunities to participate in recruiting, mentoring, and community outreach.

Recent I&D Achievements

Here are some examples of Cisco's inclusion and diversity achievements:

- The latest Pulse Survey results indicated progress in Cisco's efforts to narrow the gender gap across all business areas. The survey shows that Cisco women's job satisfaction rate has increased relative to men's and that there has been an increase in female employee satisfaction in all the survey categories.

- Cisco has virtually eliminated the gender gap in the company's voluntary attrition rate.

- I&D goals were added to the employee annual performance review form, encouraging employees to find out how they can contribute to a diverse and inclusive culture.

- Cisco now provides a resource guide for Cisco employers in the Asia Pacific region that covers disability issues. The guide includes a listing of regional disability-oriented organizations and websites, as well as policy examples and case studies.

Chapter 2

The ROI of Diversity and Inclusion

Today businesses are employing more underrepresented groups than ever before. This trend reflects an overall effort by leading corporations to both diversify the workforce and reach out to an increasingly varied marketplace. The business case for diversity and inclusion is related to growth in market share and the return on investment (ROI) for companies. Typically, companies and organizations with best-in-class D&I programs and leadership prove a better ROI and outperform in the stock market than those without.

The benefits of having a diverse employee base—in race, ethnicity, gender, ability, age, religion, veteran status, work styles, and experience—include becoming an employer of choice, enhanced creativity, and increased idea generation. A diverse employee base brings more knowledge, perspectives, and experience to the company, helping it appeal to an increasingly global customer base. Better ideas also ensure an organization's survival in a highly competitive business environment. Moreover, an encouraging and supportive atmosphere in the workplace enables companies to hire and retain highly competent employees.

Best-in-class organizations realize that diversity and inclusion is a prudent business practice that has wide-ranging benefits for both the company and its employees. Quantifying the results of the return on investment of diversity and inclusion is challenging, but organizations are finding that the business case for D&I is clear. The bottom line is that investing in D&I is a win-win situation for corporations and their employees.

In this chapter, we explore the following questions:

- How do leading corporations use diversity and inclusion to increase their bottom line?

- In what ways does diversity and inclusion enhance an organization's ability to secure the best global talent and connect to customers?

- What is the ultimate measure of diversity and inclusion's ROI?

Return on Diversity & Inclusion Investment

While D&I supports business growth to ensure a productive organization, integration is key in making diversity effective. Best-practice companies infuse diversity and inclusion throughout all business units. It is useful as a way to enrich the workforce and expand the market, and it is a business imperative for a company's market and consumers, workforce, community outreach, philanthropy, supplier base, and global community. Through all of these components, diversity and inclusion gives clear competitive strength to business.

Diversity initiatives can improve the quality of an organization's workforce and be the catalyst for a better return on investment (ROI) in human capital. The Sodexo Corporation is an example of how an organization exponentially increased its return on investment through D&I initiatives. For every $1 it has invested in mentoring, it has seen a return of $19, according to Dr. Rohini Anand, the company's senior vice president and global chief diversity officer. (See *Case Study: Sodexo* at end of chapter).

Workforce-Marketplace-Customer Connectivity

Diverse staffs drive sales. In a tough economy, the workforce-marketplace-customer connectivity has never proved more important; thus, making sure D&I is ingrained in the corporate culture is vital.

Culture, values, ethics, and multicultural understanding are essential to success. A clear statement of a company's diversity and inclusion values is necessary as well as the monitoring and enforcement of these values. There is a new pressure to address values on diversity and inclusion and the organization's social culture from potential employees, suppliers, and customers.

Building a service culture for customers requires emphasis on relationships; therefore, all the other areas such as supporting each new populace group are critical. All groups must market directly, tying in sales, in order to relate to customers and consumer products.

Building of new market share through multicultural marketing is smart for business, and targeted marketing is vital. Ethnic and multicultural marketing are growing facets of corporate diversity, thanks to the ever-evolving and compelling market demographics of America and the global economy.

Community and philanthropy should be embedded in the business goals of every best practice organization. Most companies already have an ROI tied to their initiatives within the community on the local, national, and/or global level. Now organizations are finding diverse community relations programs lead to recruiting, access of talent, sponsorships, external recognition, ties to grants, media coverage, and contact with suppliers.

Finally, suppliers should be included in the business strategy and even considered as corporate advocates and sales representatives. Supplier diversity is an area of expanding interest for corporate America and for the government. Corporations are setting ambitious goals for themselves to reach out to businesses not traditionally included in the supply chain.

Making the Business Case

Many companies struggle with effectively measuring the results of diversity and inclusion initiatives. In part, the challenge begins with determining what measures will yield the most useful information. For others, this task is difficult because they do not collect the necessary data required to measure diversity and inclusion. Diversity and inclusion programs, for example, are often considered to have "intangible" results, such as improved communication or improved teamwork, yet such improvements may have a significant impact on productivity, growth, and profits.

Clearly, at companies where measurement is of paramount importance, metrics is the path to successfully tracking results as well as identifying diversity and inclusion management concerns. The Fluor Corporation, for example, measures D&I from a standpoint of employee productivity and engagement in company performance, and that represents indirect costs or benefits to company. MGM Mirage, meanwhile, reports that the company measures diversity and inclusion performance in human resources, purchasing, construction, corporate philanthropy, and sales and marketing. The group also calculates the advertising equivalency value for editorial coverage about its diversity and inclusion practices.

And yet, for some companies, measuring the financial results of D&I is simply not done. As one HR exec says, "It's hard to quantify financial results. We don't approach diversity in terms of a dollar return on investment." Instead, a company may focus instead on recruitment and retention strategies and successes in order to analyze their diversity and inclusion initiatives.

To create your own metrics, begin by considering data from some of the following measurements:

- Equal employment opportunity and affirmative action metrics

- Employee attitude surveys

- Cultural audits

- Focus groups

- Customer surveys

- Management and employee evaluations

- Accountability and incentive assessments

- Training and education evaluations

The next step is to think even more broadly. Research shows that measures outside of human resources are typically more comprehensive and better demonstrate the business impact of diversity and inclusion management. By establishing broader organizational metrics in the following six categories, leaders can better measure the potential return on investment of D&I:

- Demographics

- Organizational culture

- Accountability

- Productivity/profitability

- Benchmarking

- Programmatic measures

The approaches to quantifying the ROI of D&I may vary from company to company, but the fundamental themes are the same. Diversity and inclusion is a macro-concept that must be embraced on a micro-level. Sustained progress requires education at the individual and company levels. That said, the most valuable assets in business are usually the ones on which a price cannot be placed: stakeholder relationships. Achieving goals depends on the ability to not only articulate them to others, but to also inspire others to raise the bar on their performance as well.

Collecting Data

Organizations measure broad aspects as well as more focused areas of diversity management—from the organization's demographic profile to race/ethnic and gender representation of different job groups and levels in the company, compared with labor market availability. To track these measures effectively, consider creating a diversity balance sheet or scorecard—along with effective evaluation processes. A scorecard can help promote support for dedicated resources for diversity and inclusion initiatives, link diversity and inclusion initiatives to organizational strategic goals and objectives, and demonstrate HR's value to the organization.

Often dependent on leadership commitment to diversity and inclusion, data collection is key to effective diversity measurement. Examples of meaningful data are:

- Level of participation in the firm's diversity and inclusion vision formulation.

- Number of underrepresented employees in formal mentoring programs who get promoted.

- Percentage of diversity objectives aligned with key strategic business objectives that are tied to bonus and compensation systems.

- Representation on the board of directors.

- Overall organizational climate and culture ratings and their effects on all represented groups.

As discussed, many intangible variables are linked to diversity and inclusion results. (See figure 1.) By following five basic steps, monetary values for intangible results can be established:

1. Identify a unit of measure that represents a unit of improvement.

2. Determine the value of each unit.

3. Calculate the change in performance data.

4. Determine an annual amount for the change.

5. Calculate the total value of the improvement.

Typical Intangible Variables Linked With Diversity and Inclusion

Attitude Survey Data	Employee Transfers
Organizational Commitment	Customer Satisfaction Survey Data
Climate Survey Data	Customer Complaints
Employee Complaints	Customer Response Time
Grievances	Teamwork
Discrimination Complaints	Cooperation
Stress Reduction	Conflict
Employee Turnover	Decisiveness
Employee Tardiness	Communication

Source: The Diversity Scorecard: Evaluating the Impact of Diversity on Organizational Performance, 2004.

The diversity and inclusion return on investment (DIROI) should be calculated by using the diversity and inclusion initiative cost and benefits to get the benefit/cost ratio (BCR). BCR = diversity and inclusion initiative benefits ÷ diversity and inclusion initiative costs. This ratio is also referred to as a cost-to-benefit ratio. Specifically, the DIROI calculation is the net benefit of the initiative divided by its costs: DIROI% = (net initiative benefits ÷ initiative costs) x 100.

This formula is the same basic formula used to evaluate other investments in which the ROI is reported as earnings divided by the investment. For example, the initial cost of a diversity and inclusion awareness program may be $50,000. The measurable value of the program is determined to be three years. During a three-year period, the program will have a net savings of $30,000 ($10,000 per year). Since the average book value is approximately half the cost, the average investment in this case is $25,000 ($50,000 ÷ 2). The average ROI = annual savings/average investment ($10,000/$25,000) = 40%.

Conclusion

In this chapter, we:

• Examined how leading corporations use diversity and inclusion to increase their bottom line.

• Discussed the ways in which diversity and inclusion enhances an organization's ability to secure the best global talent and connect to customers.

• Shared the ultimate measure of diversity and inclusion's ROI.

Promoting the concept of diversity and inclusion in the workplace is, above all, a process of education. Organizations that report the greatest success (and fewest problems) with D&I obtain and track maximum productivity from their total workforce. The fundamental concept that people must understand is easy to grasp: Organizations that get maximum productivity from a wide variety of people tend to perform better than those organizations that don't.

Effective diversity and inclusion measures and evaluation processes that determine the potential ROI of diversity and inclusion management can provide an organization with invaluable information to support key business imperatives—such as the impact of diversity and inclusion training and areas of improvement needed for recruitment strategies. Further, D&I initiatives that receive public acknowledgment through awards help attract bright talent and positively affect company brand and reputation.

That said, companies or products that claim they can definitively measure the exact ROI of D&I should be approached with caution. Measurement helps to make the business case for any initiatives a company may have, but for diversity and inclusion, much of what is gained by an organization may not be readily quantified. Given the rich complexity of this type of ROI, it cannot always be relegated to hard data.

Ultimately, being successful with diversity and inclusion means nurturing a culture in which all people can be happy, productive, and successful.

Chapter 3

Policy and Legal Compliance

Today, racial and ethnic diversity in the workplace is no longer optional; it is a fact of life. Diversity will continue to grow, influencing both the workplace and the marketplace. Many companies have made strides toward diversifying their workplaces. However, little progress has been made at senior levels.

The American workplace and marketplace have changed rapidly and significantly in terms of the diversity of employees and customers in the past fifty years. What was once exclusively an arena for white males, the U.S. workforce, has evolved to encompass individuals from all walks of life. And with the U.S. Census Bureau estimating that our country will have a "majority minority" population by 2050, marketplace demands will continue to shift accordingly.

Given the rapid shifts in our cultural landscape both in the United States and abroad, many corporations have moved the diversity and inclusion needle beyond compliance to systematic integration. After all, as discussed in previous chapters, diversity and inclusion benefits an organization across all areas and functions—from recruitment, retention, and advancement to sales, marketing, and community relations. Yet, before an organization can fully realize the power of D&I on its growth and bottom line, it must first build a strong foundation for D&I through legal compliance.

In this chapter, we will explore the following questions:

- How are Equal Employment Opportunity (EEO) and affirmative action different, and what are the major components of each?

- What are the legal ramifications of EEO, affirmative action, and other federal mandates on the workplace?

- What are the different types of compliance reviews?

- What are some corporate examples of EEO and affirmative action statements?

EEO and Affirmative Action: Understanding the Difference

Equal Employment Opportunity represents a body of law that prohibits discrimination on the basis of race, color, national origin, gender, religion, age, and disability. Enforced by the U.S. Equal Employment Opportunity Commission (EEOC), there are seven federal laws that are at the core of EEO law.

- **Title VII of the Civil Rights Act of 1964** was enacted by Congress to prohibit employment discrimination based on race, sex, color, religion, and national origin. Title VII applies to private employers, labor unions, and employment agencies. The Act prohibits discrimination in recruitment, hiring, wages, assignment, promotions, benefits, discipline, discharge, layoffs, and almost every aspect of employment. Title VII of the Civil Rights Act became a very powerful legislative tool which enabled much of the diversity present in today's workforce.

- **The Equal Pay Act of 1963** prohibits discrimination in the payment of wages on the basis of gender. The legislation recognized the disparity in pay between men and women doing the same or similar jobs.

- **The Age Discrimination in Employment Act of 1967** prohibits discrimination against persons who are 40 years of age or older. Prior to 1967, Congress found clear evidence of older workers being discriminated against in trying to obtain employment or being disproportionately affected by layoffs and downsizing.

- **The Americans with Disabilities Act of 1990 (ADA),** Titles I and V, as amended by the Americans with Disabilities Act Amendments Act of 2008 (ADAAA), prohibits private employers, state and local governments, employment agencies, and labor unions from discriminating against qualified individuals with disabilities in job application procedures, hiring, firing, advancement, compensation, job training, and other terms, conditions, and privileges of employment. Prior to the ADA, people with disabilities had no legal recourse with which to combat discrimination. The ADAAA, meanwhile, is intended to overturn a series of Supreme Court decisions that interpreted the Americans with Disabilities Act of 1990 in a way that made it difficult to prove that an impairment is a "disability." The ADAAA makes significant changes to the ADA's definition of "disability" that broadens the scope of coverage under both the ADA and Section 503 of the Rehabilitation Act.

- **The Rehabilitation Act of 1973,** in Sections 501 and 505, prohibits the Federal Government as an employer from discriminating against qualified individuals with disabilities.

- **The Civil Rights Act of 1991** was enacted to "strengthen and improve Federal civil rights laws, to provide for damages in cases of intentional employment discrimination, to clarify provisions regarding disparate impact actions and other purposes." Congress enacted the legislation in response to several Supreme Court decisions rendered in the late 1980s that had made it more difficult for plaintiffs to prevail in their employment discrimination suits and to recover fees and costs when they won their lawsuits.

- **The Genetic Information Nondiscrimination Act of 2008 (GINA)**, Title II, prohibits employment discrimination based on genetic information about an applicant, employee, or former employee.

EEOC enforces all of these laws and provides oversight and coordination of all federal equal employment opportunity regulations, practices, and policies. Other federal laws, not enforced by EEOC, also prohibit discrimination and reprisal against federal employees and applicants. For example, the Civil Service Reform Act of 1978 (CSRA) contains a number of prohibitions, known as prohibited personnel practices, which are designed to promote overall fairness in federal personnel actions. The CSRA prohibits any employee who has authority to take certain personnel actions from discriminating for or against employees or applicants for employment on the bases of race, color, national origin, religion, sex, age or disability. It also provides that certain personnel actions cannot be based on attributes or conduct that do not adversely affect employee performance, such as marital status and political affiliation. The Office of Personnel Management (OPM) has interpreted the prohibition of discrimination based on conduct to include discrimination based on sexual orientation. The CSRA also prohibits reprisal against federal employees or applicants for whistle-blowing, or for exercising an appeal, complaint, or grievance right. The CSRA is enforced by both the Office of Special Counsel (OSC) and the Merit Systems Protection Board (MSPB).

Affirmative Action

Affirmative Action was established by then-President Lyndon B. Johnson's Executive Order 11246 in 1965 as a way to remedy historic and continuing discrimination. Through the order, Johnson's goal was to create "not just equality as a right and a theory, but equality as a fact and as a result."

Executive Order 11246 required employers to analyze their organization's workforce composition and prepare written plans to eliminate underrepresentation of minorities and women if it existed in the workplace. These plans often set goals and timetables for increasing diversity within the organization, and to achieve the goals, recruitment, set-asides, and preference were often used.

Affirmative Action generates strong emotions and opinions both for and against the policy. Those who support the policy point to continuing disparities in pay and promotion for minorities and women in the workplace, while opponents argue that the policy runs counter to its very purpose by allowing so-called "reverse discrimination." Whatever one's opinion, few would deny that affirmative action policies have played a significant role in increasing the number of women and minorities in the workplace.

EEO laws and Affirmative Action policies were both intended to "level the playing field" in the workplace. They both help to increase diversity within organizations; however, they have limited impact on changing the culture of those organizations. Building upon the numerical gains made possible by EEO and Affirmative Action, today's diversity and inclusion initiatives focus on building inclusive workplace cultures so that all employees are able to fully contribute their skills and talents toward organizational goals.

Major differences between EEO/Affirmative Action and D&I Initiatives include:

EEO/Affirmative Action	Diversity and Inclusion Initiatives
Focus on compliance with legal mandates	Focus on organizationally-driven goals and strategies
Deficit-based approach to change	Strength-based approach to change
Focus on quantitative change	Focus on quantitative and qualitative transformation
Responsibility and accountability not vested in all leaders	Organization-wide responsibility and accountability
Seeks to improve employee demographics	Seeks to build competitive advantage

Affirmative Action is a commitment to ensure equality. It provides legal remedies to address the historic discrimination that disadvantaged groups and individuals have faced. The recordkeeping, analysis, and auditing disciplines that are cornerstones of Affirmative Action compliance are also critical tools for building diversity and inclusion policies. These tools can be used to hold management accountable.

Equal Employment Opportunity ensures protection from discrimination. EEO laws prohibit discrimination based on sex, race, religion, national origin, and/or disability/ physical ability. Legal compliance is still an issue; however, some lawsuits have led to the establishment of some strong diversity and inclusion programs with high-level chief diversity officers. Today, it is common for corporate diversity and inclusion policies go beyond EEO requirements. Exceeding the government's requirements of EEO and Affirmative Action is fundamental to the diversity and inclusion mission. Most organizations profiled in this Primer go far beyond federal agencies' requirements and set high compliance goals.

The following questions may help you to evaluate your company's compliance with EEO standards:

- What is your data system for compliance?

- How does the system work with your own EEO and compliance data?

- How do you review your numbers?

- How do you follow the new initiatives at the EEO Commission?

- What are your internal legal redress or arbitration efforts?

Legal Issues and Diversity

Working with legal counsel in a positive way is a critical part of diversity and inclusion. The general counsel will typically help design and approve procedures and redress mechanisms. All effective diversity and inclusion programs work in partnership with the general counsel office.

A legal background in the diversity and inclusion office is essential. Many diversity and inclusion officers are lawyers by training or have legal backgrounds. They know the importance of developing a positive relationship with the legal department as well as understanding policies and programs.

Roles and issues for legal and general counsel to take on with diversity and inclusion include (but are not limited to):

- EEO program, policies, and procedures

- Development and support of work/life policies and programs

- Policy development concerning LGBT to age discrimination and disability rights

- Complaint and resolution frameworks

- Legal issues (e.g. such as investigations in the workplace)

- Personnel fairness issues from discrimination suits to misconduct

- Preventive action on claims and suits

- Legal redress mechanisms

- Non-legal mechanisms for resolution

- Educational policies on how claims and systems work

- Investigation and resolution of claims (e.g. age discrimination to racial discrimination or religious and disability discrimination)

- Matrix use for representation

- Special work (e.g. immigration issues and policies)

- Application of legal issues to the global framework

- Active support of affirmative action and other key issues requiring legal action (e.g. signing amicus briefs)

- Working with the government on diversity and inclusion issues

- Development and use of supplier diversity programs and procedures

- Program support with policies and procedures

Analyzing EEO

Seyfarth Shaw, a New York-based law firm well-known for its labor and employment practice, provided the following matrix of key criteria for evaluating representation. These criteria point to tools your organization may already be using to meet its compliance obligations. With some re-orientation, these tools may aid diversity and inclusion management.

Analyze	Affirmative Action Tool	Diversity Tool
What is the race/gender composition of each of our functions or departments?	Work Force Analysis	Functional Composition Analysis
Is there diverse representation within each of our significantly-sized job classifications?	Job Group Analysis	Job Classification Composition Analysis
What is the availability of minorities and females in our internal and external talent pools?	Availability Analysis	Demographic Studies, Use of Economic Census Data, and Talent Pool Composition Analysis
What are our key internal and external talent pools?	Feeder Pool Identification	Talent Pool Identification
Are there important internal or external talent pools we are not maximizing?	Analysis of Recruitment Sources	Expansion of Talent Identification
Are our internal and external applicant pools diverse?	Review of Applicant Flow	Talent Pool Composition Analysis
If our applicant pools have diverse race/gender representation, are our placements (hires and promotions) proportionally diverse?	Separate Impact Ratio Analyses for Hiring and Promotion	Combined Adverse Impact Analysis for all Placements
Are we challenging ourselves with goals for diverse representation?	Goal-Setting at Compliance, Minimum of Two Standard Deviations from Availability	Stretch Goals at Level of Availability, Talent Pool Composition, or Other
If our workforce has diverse representation, are our reductions in force and other terminations proportionate?	Impact Ratio Analysis for Terminations	Separate Adverse Impact Analyses for RIFs, Other Involuntary Terminations, and Voluntary Terminations

© Seyfarth Shaw Affirmative Action Consulting Team

Important New Legal Trends

Color Discrimination
Discrimination based on race is illegal and is comprehensively covered by law. An increasing problem, however, is the rise in discrimination based on color. Color discrimination refers to discrimination within racial groups based on skin color, such as African Americans discriminating against other African Americans or Hispanics against other Hispanics based

on their origins or skin shade. These color-discrimination complaints pit minorities and others against members of their own races or ethnic groups. While color discrimination filings have risen within the EEOC, these filings do not indicate that they are necessarily racially-based.

This "appearance discrimination" could become a bigger problem as America's demographics change and more individuals classify themselves as multi-racial. Lawyers and the EEOC say that "appearance discrimination" will seriously affect employment in America if the issue is not addressed promptly.

Anti-discrimination training is expanding everywhere, especially for service workers. Policies are also changing as color discrimination is increasingly added to corporate harassment and discrimination policies.

Offerings of Law Firms in Diversity
The past decade has seen a dramatic increase in employment law and comprehensive legal diversity support.

- **Governance, hiring, and career development.** Like corporate America, law firms have developed their own plans and programs to move women and minorities "in and up." Now, 50% of law school graduates are women; however, representation of women in partnership ranks remains much lower. Still, law firms are learning how to meet the needs of women partners with work/life benefits. Meanwhile, recruiting more minorities is a top goal and retention areas remain a concern.

- **More law firms are building diversity counseling practices.** Some of the largest firms have recognized diversity practice groups and many more are naming practices. Workplace compliance, EEO, and Affirmative Action are keeping major law firms busy. Employment lawyers counsel clients on ensuring compliance with federal, state, and local EEO laws. They work with the Office of Federal Contract Compliance Programs (OFCCP) to support compliance. They assist with audits and litigation and "litigation avoidance." Compliance, reporting, monitoring, and, where necessary, negotiation or litigation is legal support's primary responsibilities.

Employment lawyers and law firm associates also conduct training on issues such as LGBT policies, disability policies, and older worker policies. They train in-house counsel, management, and those responsible for HR, diversity and inclusion, and recruitment functions. Also important to consider:

- **Legal support is important in government contract work.** Lawyers help to support regulatory, administrative, and compliance work as well as procurement compliance, which is a growing area. This may involve helping a company identify government contract opportunities. Law firms also assist companies with small business contract and sub-contract planning, implementation, and reporting.

- **Litigation and litigation avoidance or alternative dispute resolutions.** Law firms tackle litigation when it is essential, but lawyers are also spending far more time in litigation avoidance or alternative dispute resolution.

- **Immigration and global rights.** Immigration law and global rights are important in today's multinational companies. Special expertise is often required.

- **Audit assistance.** Outside legal help is recommended on a periodic basis.

Federal Requirements Regarding Affirmative Action
Provided by Seyfarth Shaw LLP:

Federal government contractors and subcontractors are required to act affirmatively in employing and promoting employees who are in protected groups based on race, color, religion, sex, national origin, mental or physical disability, and veteran status.

Employers Covered

Affirmative action laws and regulations are applicable to employers who have federal contracts. The following definitions are contained in Office of Federal Contract Compliance Programs (OFCCP) regulations:

Government Contracts

A government contract is any agreement between any governmental agency and any person to furnish supplies or services, or for the use of real or personal property, including lease arrangements. The term "services" includes:

- Utilities
- Construction
- Transportation
- Research
- Insurance
- Fund depository services.

Government contracts do not include agreements covering an employer/employee relationship. Federally-assisted construction contracts are separately defined.

Contractors

"Contractor" includes any prime contractor or subcontractor. A "prime contractor" means any "person" holding a contract with a federal contracting agency. A "subcontractor" is defined as any person entering into an agreement or arrangement with a contractor to furnish supplies or services or for the use of real or personal property, including lease arrangements:

- Which are necessary to the performance of any government contract or

- Under which any part of the contractor's obligation under a government contract is performed.

Additionally, an organization having no federal contracts or subcontracts itself nevertheless may be considered a federal contractor or subcontractor if it is closely related to an entity that is a contractor or subcontractor (for example a parent/subsidiary). The OFCCP considers the following factors to determine whether two organizations are a single entity or independently operated corporate affiliates:

- Common ownership

- Common directors/officers

- Exercise of control by one over the other

- Unity of personnel policies emanating from a common source

- Interdependency of operations

Under the OFCCP regulations, contractors and subcontractors may request a waiver from affirmative action requirements with respect to certain facilities that are in all respects separate and distinct from the activities of the entity with the federal contract.

Executive Order 11246

Executive Order 11246 (E.O. 11246) prohibits federal government contractors and subcontractors from discriminating in employment on the basis of race, color, religion, national origin, or sex, and requires affirmative action with respect to minorities and females to ensure nondiscrimination.

Rehabilitation Act of 1973

Section 503 of the Rehabilitation Act prohibits federal government contractors and subcontractors from discriminating against applicants or employees with mental or physical disabilities, and requires affirmative action to ensure nondiscrimination in employment decisions regarding such individuals.

Vietnam Era Veterans Readjustment Assistance Act of 1974 (VEVRAA)

Section 402 of VEVRAA, as amended by the Veterans Employment Opportunities Act of 1998, prohibits federal government contractors and subcontractors from discriminating against veterans with disabilities, veterans of the Vietnam Era, and other veterans who served on active duty during a war or in a campaign or expedition for which a campaign badge has been authorized, and requires affirmative action to ensure non-discrimination in employment decisions regarding such individuals.

Enforcement

Executive Order 11246, Section 503 of the Rehabilitation Act of 1973, and Section 402 of VEVRAA are administered by the Office of Federal Contract Compliance Programs (OFCCP), an agency of the United States Department of Labor. The OFCCP publishes regulations implementing these laws and conducts periodic compliance evaluations of federal government contractors and subcontractors. Additionally, the OFCCP investigates and handles complaints of discrimination.

Equal Opportunity Clause

Under E.O. 11246, Section 503 of the Rehabilitation Act, and Section 402 of VEVRAA, a contractor or subcontractor with a government contract or contracts exceeding $10,000 must include in its contracts an Equal Opportunity Clause. Contracts and subcontracts for indefinite quantities that are reasonably believed to exceed $10,000 are also subject to this requirement. In the Equal Opportunity Clause, the contractor must agree:

- Not to discriminate and to take affirmative action to ensure that applicants and employees are treated without regard to their race, color, religion, sex, or national origin, and to inform employees and applicants of this non-discrimination by posting notices

- To state in its solicitations and advertisements that all qualified applicants will receive consideration for employment without regard to race, color, religion, sex, or national origin

- To send a notice to any collective bargaining representative of its employees regarding the contractor's commitments under E.O. 11246

- To comply with the provisions of E.O. 11246 and the rules, regulations, and relevant orders of the secretary of labor

- To furnish all information and reports required and to permit access to records by the secretary of labor for purposes of determining compliance

- That in the event of non-compliance with the rules and regulations, the contract may be canceled, suspended, terminated, the contractor may be declared ineligible for future contracts, and such other sanctions may be imposed as provided by the order, rules and regulations, or by law

- To include the provisions of the Equal Opportunity Clause in contracts and purchase orders so that it will be binding upon subcontractors and vendors, and to consent to OFCCP action against subcontractors

Federal Rules for Contractors and Subcontractors

Listing Job Openings

Under VEVRAA, contractors and subcontractors have an additional requirement to list all employment openings with the local state job service (which could be the unemployment office) except executive and top management positions, positions that will be filled from within the contractor's organization, and positions lasting three days or less.

Recordkeeping

Federal contractors are also required to keep personnel or employment records for at least two years from the making of the record or from the personnel action involved, whichever date is later, except:

- Contractors with fewer than 150 employees, or

- Contractors without a government contract of at least $150,000 who need only keep employment and personnel records for one year

Records that need to be retained include records made or kept on or after December 22, 1997 that pertain to:

- Hiring and assignment

- Demotion, transfer, lay off, and termination

- Rates of pay and other terms of compensation

- Selection for training or apprenticeship

- Records having to do with requests for reasonable accommodation

- Results of any physical examinations

- Job advertisements and postings

- Applications and resumes

- Tests and test results

- Interview notes

Failure to keep such records amounts to non-compliance by the contractor and may lead to a presumption that the contractor has failed to keep or retain such records because the information would have been unfavorable to the contractor.

Affirmative Action Plan Development

Every contractor or subcontractor who has 50 or more employees and meets one or more of the criteria listed below is required to develop a written Affirmative Action Program (AAP) covering employment of minorities and females for each of its establishments. Each AAP must be updated annually.

The contractor either:

- Has a contract for $50,000 or more;

- Has government bills of lading which in any 12-month period, total or can reasonably be expected to total $50,000 or more; or

- Serves as a depository for government funds in any amount; or

- Is a financial institution that is an issuing and paying agent for U.S. savings bonds and savings notes in any amount.

Each physically separate facility is considered an "establishment" and must have its own AAP, with limited exceptions, as follows:

- "Functional AAPs" include an entire business function or line of business, without regard to the geographic locations of the establishments or employees in the function or line. However, any contractor who wishes to develop functional AAPs must gain approval from the OFCCP.

- If there are less than 50 employees at the establishment, the contractor can choose from three options:

    - That establishment, though small, can have its own AAP;

    - The employees can be placed in the AAP of the establishment where their human resources function resides; or

    - The employees can be placed in the AAP of the establishment where their manager is located.

AAP Contents

The OFCCP regulations set forth the required contents of an AAP. An AAP must include the following quantitative analyses:

- Organizational profile
- Job group analysis
- Placement of incumbents in job groups
- Determining availability
- Comparing incumbency to availability
- Placement goals

In addition, an AAP must include the following components:

- Designation of responsibility for implementation
- Identification of problem areas
- Action-oriented programs
- Periodic internal audits

The following is a brief description of these AAP requirements:

Quantitative AAP Requirements

An organizational profile is a depiction of the staffing pattern within an establishment. The profile provides an overview of the workforce at the establishment that may assist in identifying organizational units where women or minorities are underrepresented or concentrated. The contractor must use either the organizational display or the workforce analysis as its organizational profile:

- Organizational display. An organizational display is a detailed graphical or tabular chart, text, spreadsheet, or similar presentation of the contractor's organizational structure. The organizational display must identify each organizational unit in the establishment, and show the relationship of each organizational unit to the other organizational units in the establishment. For each organizational unit, the organizational display must indicate the following:

  › The name of the unit

  › The job, title, gender, race, and ethnicity of the unit supervisor (if the unit has a supervisor)

  › The total number of male and female incumbents

> › The total number of male and female incumbents in each of the following groups: African Americans, Hispanics, Asians/Pacific Islanders, and American Indians/ Alaskan Natives

- Workforce analysis. A workforce analysis is a listing of each job title, ranked from the lowest paid to the highest paid within each department or other similar organizational unit. The list must include departmental or unit supervision.

- If there are separate work units or lines of progression within a department, a separate list must be provided for each such work unit, or line, including unit supervisors.

- Where there are no formal progression lines or usual promotional sequences, job titles should be listed by department, job families, or disciplines, in order of wage rates or salary ranges.

- For each job title, the number of incumbents, the total number of male and female incumbents, and the total number of male and female incumbents in each of the following groups must be given: African Americans, Hispanics, Asians/Pacific Islanders, and American Indians/Alaskan Natives. The wage rate or salary range for each job title must be listed.

Job Group Analysis

A job group analysis is the first step in the contractor's comparison of the representation of minorities and women in its workforce with the estimated availability of minorities and women qualified to be employed.

In the job group analysis, jobs at the establishment with similar content, wage rates, and opportunities must be combined to form job groups. The job group analysis must include a list of the job titles that comprise each job group. The contractor must separately state the percentage of minorities and the percentage of women it employs in each job group.

All jobs located at an establishment must be reported in the job group analysis of that establishment, unless:

- There is an approved functional AAP.

- The establishment has less than 50 employees.

- Employees who work at a different establishment than their manager must be included in the AAP of their manager.

- "Corporate initiative" employees must be included in the AAP for the establishment where their selection was made.

Annotations must be added, as follows:

- If the job group analysis contains jobs that are located at another establishment, the job group analysis must be annotated to identify the actual location of those jobs.

- If the establishment at which the jobs actually are located maintains an AAP, the job group analysis of that AAP must be annotated to identify the AAP in which the jobs are included.

- If a contractor has a total workforce of fewer than 150 employees, the contractor may prepare a job group analysis using EEO-1 categories as job groups.

Determining Availability

Availability is an estimate of the number of qualified minorities or women available for employment in a given job group, expressed as a percentage of all qualified persons available for employment in the job group. The contractor must separately determine the availability of minorities and women for each job group.

In determining availability, a contractor must consider at least the following factors:

- **External availability.** The percentage of minorities or women with requisite skills in the reasonable recruitment area. The reasonable recruitment area is defined as the geographical area from which the contractor usually seeks or reasonably could seek workers to fill the positions in question. In most instances, for external availability, contractors use U.S. census data to reflect the pool of minorities and females in the labor market. In order to produce a meaningful AAP with realistic goals, it is critical that contractors use census data for geographical areas (for example, county, primary metropolitan statistical area and state) from which their employees are actually recruited and hired. Contractors should select occupational data most similar to the jobs identified in each job group.

- **Internal availability.** The percentage of minorities or women among those promotable, transferable, and trainable within the contractor's organization. For internal availability, to calculate the pool of minorities and women available within the contractor's organization, the contractor should analyze the minority and female composition of job titles or job groups in their own workforce that are the source of promotions and transfers into each job group. Where promotions and transfers occur from many areas, the contractor may calculate a weighted percentage from the combined areas or groups.

The final steps in the availability analysis are to weight each of these factors according to its importance in filling openings in the job group, multiply the assigned weight by the minority and female availability data, and then total these numbers to reach a final availability for minorities and females for each job group. These availability figures (which vary by job group) form the basis for the comparison with the existing minority and female employment to determine whether minorities and women are underutilized for a given job group and whether goals must be established.

Comparing Incumbency to Availability

This step, often referred to as the "utilization analysis," reflects a comparison of the percentages of minority and female incumbents in each job group to the final availability percentages for each job group to determine whether any job group is underutilized. The OFCCP accepts several different methods for determining underutilization, including:

- The 80% rule: whether the incumbent percentage is less than 80% of availability for each job group

- The "any difference" rule: whether there is any difference between the percentages of incumbent minorities and females and availability percentages

- The two standard deviation rule: whether the difference exceeds two standard deviations

- The "one person" rule: whether the difference exceeds one person

If, upon using one of these methods, minority or female underutilization is found in any job group, the contractor must establish a placement goal.

Placement Goals

Placement goals serve as objectives or targets that can be attained by applying good faith efforts. Placement goals also are used to measure progress toward achieving equal employment opportunity.

A contractor's determination that a placement goal is required constitutes neither a finding nor an admission of discrimination.

Where a contractor is required to establish a placement goal for a job group, it must establish a percentage annual placement goal equal to the availability figure derived for women or minorities for that job group.

Contractors should establish a single goal for all minorities. In the event of a substantial disparity in the utilization of a particular minority group, a contractor may be required by the OFCCP to establish separate goals.

In establishing placement goals, the following principles also apply:

- Placement goals may not be rigid and inflexible quotas, which must be met, nor are they to be considered as either a ceiling or a floor for the employment of particular groups. Quotas are expressly forbidden.

- In all employment decisions, the contractor must make selections in a non-discriminatory manner. Placement goals do not provide the contractor with a justification to extend a preference to any individual, select an individual, or adversely affect an individual's employment status on the basis of that person's race, color, religion, sex, or national origin.

- Placement goals do not create set-asides for specific groups, nor are they intended to achieve proportional representation or equal results.

- Placement goals may not be used to supersede merit selection principles. AAPs do not require a contractor to hire a person who lacks qualifications to perform the job successfully, or hire a less qualified person in preference to a more qualified one.

The contractor must provide for the implementation of equal employment opportunity and the AAP by assigning responsibility and accountability to an official of the organization. Depending upon the size of the contractor, this may be the official's sole responsibility. He or she must have the authority, resources, support of, and access to top management to ensure the effective implementation of the AAP.

Identification of Problem Areas

The contractor must perform in-depth analyses of its total employment process to determine whether and where impediments to equal employment opportunity exist. At a minimum, the contractor must evaluate:

- The workforce by organizational unit and job group to determine whether there are problems of minority or female utilization (e.g. employment in the unit or group), or of minority or female distribution (e.g. placement in the different jobs within the unit or group)

- Personnel activity (e.g. applicant flow, hires, terminations, promotions, and other personnel actions) to determine whether there are selection disparities

- Compensation system(s) to determine whether there are gender, race, or ethnicity-based disparities

- Selection, recruitment, referral, and other personnel procedures to determine whether they result in disparities in the employment or advancement of minorities or women

- Any other areas that might impact the success of the affirmative action program

Action-Oriented Programs

The contractor must develop and execute action-oriented programs designed to correct any problem areas identified and to attain established goals and objectives. In order for these action-oriented programs to be effective, the contractor must ensure that they consist of more than following the same procedures, which have previously produced inadequate results. Furthermore, a contractor must demonstrate that it has made good faith efforts to remove identified barriers, expand employment opportunities, and produce measurable results.

Internal Audit and Reporting System

The contractor must develop and implement an auditing system that periodically measures the effectiveness of its total affirmative action program. The actions listed below are key to a successful AAP:

- Monitor records of all personnel activity, including referrals, placements, transfers, promotions, terminations, and compensation, at all levels to ensure the non-discriminatory policy is carried out

- Require internal reporting on a scheduled basis as to the degree to which equal employment opportunity and organizational objectives are attained

- Review report results with all levels of management

- Advise top management of program effectiveness and submit recommendations to improve unsatisfactory performance

Achievement of Prior Year's Goals

As part of maintaining and updating the AAP annually, the contractor must prepare a report stating the prior year's goals and the extent to which they have been achieved through minority and female hires and promotions. In instances where a goal has not been achieved, it is important that the contractor discuss the good faith efforts which have been made in attempting to achieve the goal.

Affirmative Action for Individuals with a Disability and Veterans

Contractors and subcontractors are required to take affirmative action to employ and to advance in employment qualified disabled individuals, veterans with disabilities, veterans of the Vietnam era, and other covered veterans.

Definitions

The ADAAA defines a disability as:

- a physical or mental impairment that substantially limits a major life activity; or

- a record of a physical or mental impairment that substantially limited a major life activity; or

- when an entity (e.g., an employer) takes an action prohibited by the ADA based on an actual or perceived impairment.

A "disabled veteran" is a person:

- Entitled to disability compensation under laws administered by the Veterans Administration for disability rated at 30% or more of total disability
- Whose discharge or release from active duty was the result of a disability incurred or aggravated in the line of duty

A "special disabled veteran" is a veteran who:

- Is entitled to compensation (or who but for the receipt of military retired pay would be entitled to compensation) under laws administered by the Veterans Administration for a disability rated at 30% or more, or rated at 10 or 20% in the case of a veteran who has been determined under section 1506 of Title 38, U.S.C., to have a serious employment disability
- A person who was discharged or released from active duty because of a service-related disability

A "qualified disabled veteran" is a disabled veteran who is capable of performing the essential functions of his/her particular job, with or without a reasonable accommodation.

Pursuant to the Veterans Employment Opportunities Act of 1998, "other covered veterans" means other veterans who served on active duty during a war or in a campaign or expedition for which a campaign badge has been authorized.

AAPs for Individuals with Disabilities and Veterans

Contractors are required to develop AAPs for individuals with disabilities and veterans if they have 50 employees and a federal contract or subcontract of $50,000. Typically, contractors consolidate the separate AAPs for the disabled and covered veterans into a single AAP.

AAP obligations for individuals and veterans with disabilities are enforced by the OFCCP. Unlike E.O. 11246, the OFCCP regulations covering disabled and veterans AAPs do not require statistical analyses. Instead, these regulations provide detailed requirements that reflect the contractor's efforts to recruit and hire qualified disabled individuals and covered veterans.

OFCCP Review and Enforcement

The OFCCP has established a two-part enforcement process. Compliance reviews and enforcement serve to reveal and correct violations of affirmative action requirements.

OFCCP Compliance Reviews

The purpose of any compliance review is to determine a contractor's compliance with its affirmative action and equal opportunity obligations at a particular establishment. In conducting a compliance review, the OFCCP seeks to determine whether the contractor's AAP is in compliance with applicable regulations, and whether the contractor has engaged in good faith efforts during the last year to meet its affirmative action goals.

Standard Compliance Review

In the typical compliance review, the OFCCP examines whether, and to what extent, areas of potential discrimination exist at the contractor's workplace. To determine potential discrimination, the OFCCP uses adverse impact analyses in an attempt to determine whether statistically significant differences exist with respect to the contractor's selection of minorities and women for hire, promotion, transfer, demotion, layoff, recall, and/or termination, indicating a pattern or practice of discrimination. A statistically significant difference, generally, is a less than 80% selection of (or more than two standard deviation differences between) minorities or women compared to the non-minority or male group.

Desk Audit

The compliance review begins when the contractor receives a standard letter from the OFCCP containing notice of the review and a request for the contractor's AAP and supporting data such as logs of applicants, hires, transfers, promotions, terminations EEO-1 reports, organizational charts, workforce analysis, utilization analysis, and goals for underutilized areas. After receiving these materials, the OFCCP compliance officer will review the data for completeness and accuracy, and determine whether the contractor has complied with the regulations.

Additionally, the compliance officer will review past goal achievement, identify areas exhibiting concentration or under-representation of minorities and females, and attempt to identify affected classes. An impact ratio analysis (IRA) is conducted at this stage to identify areas needing further investigation. If an impact ratio analysis indicates a less favorable selection rate of women and minorities, it is used as a preliminary indicator of potential discrimination. The OFCCP also reviews the contractor's compensation analyses and conducts its own analysis to determine whether evidence of individual or class wide disparate treatment against women or minorities is present.

The compliance officer also may contact other agencies to review discrimination complaints against the contractor and to determine the contractor's reputation for nondiscrimination in the community. For this purpose, the compliance officer may contact community agencies, recruiting sources, and referral sources, including state employment services.

On-site Audit

Many compliance reviews include an on-site audit that involves a visit by the compliance officer to the contractor's facility to investigate problem areas revealed during the desk audit. The on-site audit typically includes the following:

- An entrance conference in which the compliance officer meets with the chief executive officer or designee

- A review of employment policies and procedures

- A review of personnel records, including computerized records, focusing on personnel practices having an adverse impact or causing concentrations or under-representation

- A tour of the facility to survey general working conditions, accommodations to disabled applicants and employees, and the presence of required postings

- Interviews with women and minority employees regarding their opportunities for advancement. Interviews may also be conducted with minorities or women who have current EEOC complaints, have information concerning some area of substantive deficiency, have been refused a promotion, work in entry-level jobs, or appear to be members of a potentially affected class

- Interviews with managers and supervisors in work units with concentrations or under-representations of women and/or minorities or other substantial deficiencies (the employer's representative or attorney may be present)

- A review of training and educational programs, compensation practices, grievance, disciplinary and termination procedures, and technical requirements such as inclusion of the EEO caption on recruiting material, inclusion of the Equal Opportunity Clause in purchase orders and contracts, submission of the EEO-1 report, and notification to vendors and subcontractors of equal employment requirements

- Review of I-9 compliance

- An exit conference with the CEO or designee that the employer should use to obtain a thorough understanding of the OFCCP findings, including problem areas and areas requiring further off-site analysis

Off-Site Review

An off-site review of records is intended to provide an analysis and evaluation of the affirmative action plan and supporting documents to determine whether the contractor is in compliance with affirmative action requirements.

Focused Review

A focused review is an on-site review restricted to one or more components of the contractor's organization or one or more aspects of the contractor's employment practices.

Compliance Check

A compliance check is an alternative, expedited means of screening records to ensure that a contractor is in compliance with recordkeeping and retention requirements. The compliance check begins with a scheduling letter that usually provides the contractor a short (often as little as a few days) notice period before the check. The actual check consists of an inspection of the contractor's documents to ensure that the contractor is maintaining required documents regarding:

- Achievement of goals set in the prior year's AAP

- A listing of accommodations provided to disabled applicants and employees'

- Examples of employment advertising including the "equal opportunity employer" M/F/D/V tag line

- Documentation of the listing of job openings with the local employment office.

After the compliance officer has completed the investigation portion of the compliance check, the contractor will receive a closure letter.

Glass Ceiling or Corporate Management Reviews

The term "glass ceiling" refers to invisible barriers blocking women and minorities from advancing up the corporate ladder to management- and executive-level positions. These barriers may include stereotyping or bias, poor internal employment-related data collection and analysis, insufficient outreach and recruitment practices, lack of mentoring and management training, as well as lack of opportunities for career development.

To correct the noted absence of women and minorities in upper level management positions, the OFCCP conducts Corporate Management Reviews (also referred to as "glass ceiling" reviews). The reviews focus on corporate headquarters and include an evaluation of whether women or minorities suffer disparate treatment in selection, advancement, compensation, or other employment-related matters, especially at senior levels and in the positions that constitute the "pipeline" for the senior positions. The OFCCP may choose to extend the scope of the review beyond corporate headquarters. During such "glass ceiling" reviews, the OFCCP usually conducts the following seven processes and procedures:

1. An entrance conference with the CEO

2. A review of jobs by both management title and by salary level

3. An assessment of each functional area in the company and the concentration of women and minorities in each area. Particularly important is whether women and minorities are in staff positions within each area that lead to management promotions and executive positions

4. A review of internal recruiting pools to determine whether such pools are materially different in composition from higher-level jobs, and, if so, whether women and minorities are concentrated in job areas that do not feed into management positions

5. A review of external recruitment and hiring processes, including a review of announcements or advertisements, applicant flow, and dissemination of the affirmative action policy, particularly if an external recruiting firm is screening applicants for the employer or if word of mouth recruiting is used for senior positions

6. A review of related employment matters, such as exposure to senior management and compensation packages for women and minorities as compared to others at the same level, and

7. On-site investigations and interviews, including interviews of the CEO, senior executives, and the most highly compensated women and minorities; a review of compensation; structure and administration; management succession plans; and applicant resumes. An employer is entitled to have an attorney or representative present if a review officer interviews management or supervisory employees, but not if the review officer interviews other employees.

The review will conclude with an exit conference with the CEO to discuss violations and options.

Violations

If a compliance officer finds a violation in any type of compliance review, the following steps may be taken depending upon the contractor's willingness to cooperate with the OFCCP:

- Negotiation of a conciliation agreement wherein the contractor agrees to correct major violations by precise actions or a precise time table with reporting obligations and including, where appropriate, remedies such as back pay and retroactive seniority or

- Referral for consideration of formal enforcement

Where a conciliation agreement is violated the following steps may be taken:

- The OFCCP sends written notice to the contractor of the violation and supporting evidence

- The contractor has 15 days to respond unless affected employees or applicants would suffer irreparable injury in that time

- The contractor attempts to "show cause" that it has not violated the agreement. (Note, the OFCCP may bring an enforcement action on the conciliation agreement without presenting proof of underlying violations resolved by the agreement) and

- Enforcement proceedings

Enforcement Proceedings

At any time during the course of the compliance review, if the OFCCP has reasonable cause to believe that a contractor has violated the law, it may issue a "show-cause" notice requiring the contractor to explain, within 30 days, why monitoring, enforcement proceedings, or other appropriate action by the OFCCP to ensure compliance should not be instituted. Enforcement proceedings, which are similar to a trial, will be initiated where the contractor:

- Fails to submit an affirmative action program and/or to establish and maintain records and information related to an affirmative action program, or

- Refuses to supply records or other requested information, or

- Refuses to allow an on-site compliance review to be conducted, or

- Fails to substantially comply with a conciliation agreement, or

- Fails to correct the alleged violation of regulations, or

- Fails to correct violations based on a complaint investigation

Enforcement proceedings may be stopped at any point if the contractor is willing to accept the OFCCP's proposed resolution or if the parties are able to negotiate a settlement.

The determination of whether to bring an enforcement action rests with an attorney within the Department of Labor, upon referral by the OFCCP. No economic sanctions can be taken against a contractor without the contractor being given an opportunity to present evidence at a hearing before an administrative law judge. Depending on the nature of the violation, the sanction sought against the contractor may include back pay and/or reinstatement or being banned from working on federal contracts, in addition to other possible penalties.

After a hearing, the administrative law judge will issue recommended findings, conclusions, and a decision. Each party may submit to the secretary of labor exceptions to the recommendation, and the secretary of labor will issue a final administrative order. The contractor may appeal an adverse decision to the appropriate federal court.

Penalties

Failure to comply with a final administrative order issued by the secretary of labor at the conclusion of the enforcement proceedings will result in sanctions against the contractor. Specifically, the secretary of labor may:

- Award back pay and interest, as well as prospective relief to an affected individual or class

- Withhold payments due under a contract until the violation is corrected

- Cancel or terminate the contract

- Bar the contractor from receiving future contracts for a fixed or indefinite period of six months to three years

- Notify all federal contracting agencies of this bar

- Seek to prevent others from entering into contracts with the contractor

- Recommend that the EEOC or Department of Justice institute appropriate proceedings under Title VII

Conclusion

In this chapter, we:

- Reviewed the difference between Equal Employment Opportunity (EEO) and affirmative action and the major components of each.

- Discussed the legal ramifications of EEO, affirmative action, and other federal mandates on the workplace.

- Explored different types of compliance reviews.

- Shared corporate examples of EEO and affirmative action statements.

Over the last half century, compliance and affirmative action have risen to diversity and inclusion, and companies that have made a deep and steady commitment to D&I, particularly throughout the current global economic situation, have proven to be true industry leaders and community visionaries and have seen their bottom lines grow as a result.

Although compliance may not be considered a "hot" topic these days in the D&I world, high profile discrimination lawsuits continuously remind us of the importance of legal considerations when it comes to diversity and inclusion and of the severe ramifications when one does not follow the law. Moreover, while EEO and affirmative action policies were both originally created to allow for equal access to opportunity and advancement for underrepresented groups, especially for minorities and women, compliance alone does little to create an inclusive workplace where all feel valued. However, when human differences are combined in a common vision and toward a concerted effort, the benefits cannot be understated. Diversity and inclusion is the vehicle in which 21st century organizations are realizing their potential for growth, yet before D&I can be leveraged for maximum effectiveness, companies must have a strong foundation of legal compliance.

Corporate Examples:
EEO and Affirmative Action Statements

The Boeing Company

Boeing's policy on equal employment opportunity prohibits discrimination based on race, color, religion, national origin, gender, sexual orientation, gender identity, age, physical or mental disability, or veteran status. This policy applies to recruiting, hiring, transfers, promotions, terminations, compensation and benefits, and also states that retaliation against any employee who files a complaint regarding possible violations of this policy will not be tolerated.

Boeing is committed to taking affirmative steps to promote the employment and advancement of minorities, women, persons with disabilities, and covered veterans. Every year, Boeing develops affirmative action programs to support its commitment to equal employment opportunity, consistent with company policy and the company's obligations as a contractor to the United States government.

Booz Allen Hamilton

As one of our firm's Core Values, diversity is reflected in our policies. Our fundamental Equal Employment policy is "to identify, attract, retain, and advance the most qualified persons, without regard to their race, color, religion, sex, national origin, age, marital status, sexual orientation, gender identity and expression, disability, veterans status, genetic information, or any other status protected by law." In addition, we have implemented policies on Acquired Immune Deficiency Syndrome, Flexible Work Arrangements, Persons with Disabilities, US Domestic Partner Benefits, Sexual Harassment, and Workplace Harassment, among others.

Intel Corporation

At Intel, diversity is respected, valued and welcomed in the workforce, as well as in our customers, our suppliers, and the global marketplace. Our policy is to provide equal employment opportunities for all applicants and employees.

We do not discriminate on the basis of race, color, religion, sex, national origin, ancestry, age, disability, veteran status, marital status, gender identity or sexual orientation. This policy applies to all aspects and stages of employment from recruitment through retirement. It prohibits harassment of any individual or group.

KPMG

KPMG reaffirms its long-standing policy of providing equal opportunity for all applicants and employees, regardless of their race, color, creed, religion, age, gender, national origin, citizenship status, marital status, sexual orientation, gender identity, disability, pregnancy, veteran status, or other legally protected status.

This policy applies to recruiting, hiring, rates of pay and other compensation, benefits, promotions, transfers, demotions, terminations, reductions in force, disciplinary actions, and all other terms, conditions, or privileges of employment.

The New York Times Company

The New York Times Company's continuing success depends on its ability to hire qualified people and to provide our staff with a stimulating and challenging environment in which to work. Therefore, we provide equal employment opportunity for all regardless of race, color, citizenship, religion, national origin, sex, sexual orientation, gender identity or expression, age, disability, veteran or reservist status or any other category protected by federal, state or local law.

The policy of equal employment opportunity affects all employment practices including recruiting, employment assignments, training, compensation, advancement, transfers, terminations, layoffs, recalls, working conditions and benefits.

OfficeMax Inc.

OfficeMax is committed to a workplace free of discrimination and harassment based on race, color, religion, gender, national origin, age, sexual orientation, disability, veteran status, or any other protected status under federal, state or local law.

Case Study: WellPoint, Inc.

WellPoint recruits, hires, trains, and promotes persons in all job titles without regard to age, color, disability, gender (including gender identity), marital status, national origin, race, religion, sex, sexual orientation, veteran status, or other status protected by applicable law. In addition, all personnel actions such as compensation, promotion, demotion, benefits, transfers, staff reductions, terminations, reinstatement and rehire, company-sponsored training, education and tuition assistance, and social and recreational programs will be administered in accordance with the principles of equal employment opportunity.

In keeping with these principles, WellPoint is committed to providing all associates with a work environment that is free from all forms of harassment based on age, color, disability, gender, marital status, national origin, race, religion, sex, sexual orientation, veteran status, or any other characteristic protected by applicable law. WellPoint is committed to providing reasonable accommodations to qualified individuals with disabilities who can perform the essential functions of the job they hold or desire, with or without a reasonable accommodation.

WellPoint takes affirmative action to ensure equal employment opportunity for females, minorities, individuals with disabilities, and covered veterans. Each facility has an EEO coordinator who is responsible for compliance with applicable regulations regarding affirmative action. In addition, WellPoint's Equal Employment Opportunity program consultant and affirmative action consultant have primary responsibilities for coordinating and managing the success of the affirmative action program.

All associates are responsible for compliance with this policy to ensure a working environment free from discrimination and harassment. Members of management have a responsibility to prevent conducts inconsistent with this policy, to properly handle any known or reported violations, and to implement affirmative action programs within their areas of responsibility. Our policy statement embraces our core values: Customer First, Integrity, Personal Accountability for Excellence, Lead through Innovation, and One Company-One Team.

EEO Compliance Training

In December 2008, WellPoint rolled out a mandatory EEO compliance training to all managers. This comprehensive program covered all aspects of equal opportunity that are an inherent part of all management decisions that affect its associates, including hiring, promoting, compensation, transfers, staff reductions, termination, reinstatement, coaching, and feedback.

By the end of May 2009, this online course had been completed by 99 percent of its managers, ensuring that WellPoint's leaders are educated on the regulatory guidelines that govern its decision-making process and are accountable for compliance. The online training of managers was conducted in addition to the ongoing mandatory training for associates who are designated EEO coordinators and who are responsible for educating key business leaders on the importance of EEO compliance.

Procedure

The Chief Human Resources Officer has overall responsibility for implementing the Company's Affirmative Action Plan and for ensuring that all personnel actions are administered in accordance with this policy and with federal and state law.

All associates, including members of management, are equally responsible for administering and implementing affirmative action programs within their areas of responsibility and for ensuring compliance with this policy as well as federal and state statutes regulating equal employment opportunity and affirmative action.

Any associate or job applicant who believes that he or she has been subject to unlawful discrimination or discriminatory harassment on the basis of race, color, religion, sex, ancestry, age, national origin, marital status, veteran status, medical condition, disability, sexual orientation, or sexual harassment is encouraged and expected to immediately notify a local Human Resources representative. WellPoint encourages associates to take every step possible to make sure that Human Resources is informed of their concern.

There can be no threat of retaliation against the associate by the Company or another associate (including management) for reporting a discrimination or discriminatory harassment complaint.

Associates who have had a complaint of discrimination or discriminatory harassment addressed under this policy must immediately notify a local Human Resources representative if the discrimination or discriminatory harassment resumes, or the associate believes that retaliation is occurring.

All complaints involving equal employment opportunity, discrimination, or discriminatory harassment will be thoroughly investigated by Human Resources and promptly resolved. The investigation and resolution of the alleged incidents will proceed confidentially to the extent that it is reasonable and practical.

The Company will assure that the investigation is thorough, involves the appropriate management, is documented, and that the associate reporting discrimination is informed in writing at the conclusion of the investigation.

The Company shall take any and all appropriate steps, up to and including termination of employment, against associates who violate this policy.

Source: WellPoint, Inc.

Chapter 4

Culture, Values, and Ethics

Your company's culture and ethical norms are a component of its diversity and inclusion effectiveness. Increasingly, when CEOs, business leaders, and heads of business units speak out on diversity and inclusion, they are speaking out on values, culture, and ethics. These clear statements of "D&I values" are essential, as is the monitoring and enforcement of the values. Best-practice companies often readdress their values equation to make sure the mission is clear to their employees. They also further clarify their expectations on the company's website and intranet.

While some companies have already crafted a company culture founded on the principals of ethics and inclusion, current events and the ensuing national dialogue are increasing the pressure on all organizations to readdress acceptable social culture.

From awards for supplier diversity to badges for eco-friendliness and "top" lists for LGBT initiatives to spotlights for women and minority leadership, companies today are vying for employees and customers by displaying their achievements loud and clear. In the current workplace and marketplace, a company's culture, values, and ethics matter more than ever and are manifesting themselves in a variety of ways.

There is a revolutionary commitment to establish a unique company culture founded on the principals of ethics and inclusion. At the same time, current events and the ensuing national dialogue are increasing the pressure on all organizations—government, corporate, non-profit, and social service—to step up their game in regard to being employers of choice and the "go-to" places for socially conscious products and services. Through visible CEO leadership, sustainability standards, community involvement, work-life balance programs, and diversity and inclusion policies, people are sizing up companies for *who* they are, not just what they offer.

In this chapter, we will explore the following questions:

- What are the key trends in corporate culture, values, and ethics?

- What does ethical leadership "look" like?

- How does having a strong commitment to diversity and inclusion and ethical practices boost an organization's investment appeal?

- What are some corporate examples of culture, values, and ethics statements?

Trends in Culture, Values, and Ethics:

Company culture and the underlying values of the culture are understood as drivers for performance. Cultural audits and their measurements of change are critical indicators from a company's workforce. Cultural surveys, assessments, and audits are standard tool barometers for change.

To that end, companies should recommit themselves to a formal process of values developed around diversity and inclusion that is embraced across the company, including the following:

- The values the company embodies

- The company mission

- The company vision

- The ethics by which they and all employees conduct themselves

Companies are naming chief diversity officers, chief ethics officers, and chief culture officers, and in some cases are combining all three functions into a single "C-level" officer position. Meanwhile, cultural components and diversity and inclusion values are being included in employee surveys.

- 360° evaluations are being deployed from top management all the way to entry-level employees. The assessment of individuals by their colleagues, based on how they "live" diversity and inclusion values, is being established as a performance measurement that has an impact on employees incentive pay

- Employee advocacy is being added as a function and competency of the D&I and/or ethics officer

- Strong tie in from the general counsel's office to ensure that every aspect of values-related expectations is clear and cogent

- Inclusion of the company's communications team in strategy formulation

The Essence of Ethical Leadership: New Directions

The combination of D&I and ethics continues to shape business. Tying diversity and inclusion policies to ethics, social responsibility, and reputation can increase recruiting, retention, and stock price. And yet, an effective program emphasizes behavior, not just compliance. For example, at Waste Management, when the ethics officer retired, the CEO merged the ethics and diversity functions. Waste Management's CEO made it clear that the focus would be on behavior and not compliance. In the end, tying ethics to diversity did more for D&I than ever imagined within corporate management. Having the new role report directly to top leadership demonstrated the highest level of commitment.

When ethics and D&I are combined, the Board of Directors and senior management can more clearly see results. An ethics and D&I report card can also help a company measure how it is doing. Best-practice companies regularly review their codes of conduct to ensure that the ethics policy is clear. These new codes are then shared with employees—at all levels. Companies also review the help, complaint, or feedback lines to gauge response.

Investing

More investor funds are looking for socially responsible companies and are researching diversity and inclusion policies. Take, for instance, the Calvert Group's Diversity Index. From this list, corporations can recognize the impact that diversity and inclusion policies can have on stock price. Similarly, the Social Investment Forum offers comprehensive information, contacts, and resources on socially responsible investing. Other resources include the Domini Index and the Domini Social Equity Fund, and the Human Rights Campaign's HRC Corporate Equality Index, which focuses on LGBT issues such as domestic partner benefits.

Beyond these well-publicized lists, more women, minority groups, and others are forming investment clubs. These investment groups seek out companies committed to D&I and to their own interests. This issue will be a major one as the decade continues. Best-practice companies know how important it will be to do well on surveys with those tracking diversity and inclusion leadership.

Conclusion

In this chapter, we:

• Established key trends in corporate culture, values, and ethics.

• Listed components of ethical leadership.

• Explored how a strong commitment to diversity and inclusion and ethical practices boosts an organization's investment appeal.

More and more, a company's culture and its ethical norms are becoming inextricably tied to its diversity and inclusion effectiveness. Increasingly, when CEOs and business leaders speak out on diversity and inclusion, they are also speaking out on values, culture, and ethics.

Corporations are finding themselves at the center of deeply held values of their workforce and their customer base. This reality has made it that much more important for companies to clarify and project their D&I value statements as well as monitor and enforce them. On the internet, intranet, in public speeches, and through everyday actions, best-in-class companies know that who they are is becoming just as important as what they are selling.

Corporate Examples: Mission, Vision, Values

Carlton Fields, P.A.

Carlton Fields has a tradition and culture of diversity. We are committed to creating a climate of inclusion, growing our talent pool, and fostering innovation and creativity to compete in the global market. We believe that persons with diverse backgrounds enrich our work environment, add value to the legal services that we provide, and enhance the overall culture of the firm.

CDW Corporation

CDW offers an inclusive work environment that leverages diverse perspectives in order for coworkers to excel and drive CDW's success.

Just as solid and dependable technological solutions require many components to maximize capability, so does our approach to diversity and inclusion. The very name of our diversity and inclusion practice - Connections@CDW - suggests that it's all about making solid and dependable connections in the workplace, with our customers and supplier partners, and in our communities. We seek to:

- Promote a team conscience that is inclusive and reflective of the markets we serve

- Foster diverse thought and an inclusive work environment that enables each coworker to excel

- Provide our customers with the best talent to understand and meet their unique needs

- Leverage a diverse supplier network that adds value and innovation to our business

Valuing diversity is an important priority for CDW. We believe that it is more than just the right thing to do. We believe that it is critical for overall organizational health and well being.

Cisco Systems, Inc.

At Cisco, we continually strive to be a better company, and a better corporate citizen. We aim to fully embrace the human network in all its multiplicity, and to foster innovation and talent in the workplace. This way, we can better serve our customers and engage with our partners in the worldwide marketplace.

We demonstrate our commitment to a culture of inclusion and diversity by:

- Integrating inclusion and diversity into business processes and operations

- Creating systemic accountability for realizing the inclusion and diversity objectives at every level of the organization

- Increasing recognition of employees who create a culture of inclusion

- Using our pervasive culture of inclusion to attract and retain top talent

- Challenging Cisco's executive team to consistently and broadly spread the inclusion and diversity vision

- Strengthening the Cisco brand through our reputation as an inclusion and diversity leader

ConAgra Foods

At ConAgra Foods, we serve a very broad base of customers and consumers. To best serve them, we will create an organizational climate that values the diversity and unique qualities of our employees, customers, and consumer base. In doing so, ConAgra Foods is committed to an environment and employee base that:

- Reflects the growing diversity of our customers and consumers in order to serve them more successfully

- Is supported by management policies that respond to the needs of a diverse workforce, is inclusive, and enables the full contribution of every person in the organization

- Is sensitive and responsive to diversity among customers, consumers, suppliers, and communities in which we work

- Is sensitive and responsive to the work-life needs of our employees

- Promotes a sense of company responsibility on issues of diversity and inclusion

Dell, Inc.

Dell is committed to inclusion and diversity. Our mission is to succeed in the marketplace by fostering a winning culture of Dell employees who are highly talented, committed, reflective of our global customers and recognized as our greatest strength.

Dell's diversity initiatives focus on three business imperatives:

1. To provide a great customer experience, which requires a workforce reflective of our customers

2. To access the best and brightest talent the marketplace has to offer

3. To focus on global expansion with employees who understand the various cultures, giving us a competitive advantage

Diversity is at the core of Dell's values and winning culture. It helps define the kind of company we are and aspire to be. Diversity initiatives tap additional talent, retain employees, strengthen relationships, improve our operating results, and further our global citizenship efforts in the many communities we call home. Dell defines diversity in its broadest sense: "It's About Inclusion."

At Dell, we're committed to building a diverse environment that is reflective of a diverse global marketplace and an inclusive culture where everyone is engaged. We strive to ensure that each employee is heard and valued and that personal strengths and perspectives are assets to the company, rather than being left at the door.

To achieve our vision for an even more diverse and inclusive global company, we established a global diversity strategy, which is reviewed regularly by the Global Diversity Council. Our strategy focuses on:

- Strong, visible leadership commitment and clear expectations of accountability for diversity and inclusion

- Genuine commitment to diversity and inclusion built into our business practices

- Thorough integration of these behaviors in our talent and performance management

Eastman Kodak Company

Our Global Diversity Vision is an inclusive environment in which we leverage diversity to achieve company business objectives and maximize the potential of individuals and the organization.

The Mission of the Global Diversity & Community Affairs Office is to integrate diversity and inclusion in all aspects of the business in order to:

- Fully engage the energies of Kodak's employees and a diverse supplier base

- Meet competitive challenges in the marketplace

- Maximize shareholder value

Johnson Controls, Inc.

For Johnson Controls, diversity is a requirement for doing business right. We provide customers with products and services reflecting the preferences of a diverse global marketplace. This requires a workforce with the thoughts, ideas and experiences needed to serve all markets.

Johnson Controls is committed to attracting, developing and training the best talent in the world. Recognizing that excellence comes in many forms and from every region, we foster a culture that promotes excellent performance, teamwork, inclusion, leadership and growth.

To accomplish our business growth objectives, our employees must be involved and engaged as individuals and as team members. Our employee and leader diversity mirrors our global markets and population. We do that by hiring and working with smart, talented people who can bring us diverse perspectives and capabilities.

We work to eliminate discrimination and harassment in all its forms, and we are committed to providing equal opportunity in all of our employment practices. By valuing diversity, all our employees can fully realize their potential

Johnson & Johnson

Our vision is to maximize the global power of diversity and inclusion to drive superior business results and sustainable competitive advantage. We will achieve our vision by:

- Fostering credo-based inclusive cultures that embrace our differences and drive innovation to accelerate growth (workplace)

- Achieving a skilled, high performance workforce that is reflective of the diverse global marketplace (workforce)

- Working with business leaders to identify and establish targeted market opportunities for consumers across diverse demographic segments (marketplace)

- Cultivating external relationships with professional, patient and civic groups to support business priorities (external stakeholders).

Medtronic

At Medtronic, we recognize that a broad spectrum of skills, values and cultures are essential for innovation and growth. As such, significant diversity characterizes our employees, as well as our customers and their patients, and will continue to do so as Medtronic grows into the 21st Century.

We are committed to being the employer of choice for our globally diverse work force. Our goal is to respect employees and maintain a workplace where all employees can contribute to their full potential. We strive for maximum awareness, skill and adaptability in dealing with differences among employees, customers, and other stakeholders. Clarity, honesty, and directness mark our approach as we focus on fulfilling Medtronic's mission to alleviate pain, restore health, and extend life.

The New York Times Company

The New York Times Company is committed to diversity in its most inclusive sense, so it's not simply an issue of race or ethnicity. We seek to attract, develop and retain people from a rich variety of experiences, ethnic backgrounds and cultures. In a rapidly changing world, our diverse workforce will strengthen our competitive position in the global marketplace and help us to achieve our company's core purpose, which is "to enhance society by creating, collecting and distributing high quality news, information and entertainment."

The Procter & Gamble Company

P&G believes a fully engaged and leveraged diverse work force is a competitive advantage. Our goal is to grow that competitive edge by fostering an inclusive culture.

Diversity is a business strategy for P&G. It's an intentional choice that creates sustainable competitive advantage. It is implicit in the company's purpose and explicit in the company's business strategy for success. We simply cannot create brands and products to improve the lives of the world's consumers unless we deeply understand and value the diversity of their needs and aspirations. We believe the best way to do this is to have a work force that reflects the markets and consumers we serve and to fully value and leverage all of their experiences, insights and talents. That's why P&G's corporate diversity strategy is: Everyone valued, Everyone included, Everyone performing at their peak.

Trinity Health

Trinity Health operates dozens of hospitals and hundreds of health centers in seven states. Because we serve diverse populations, our associates are trained to recognize the cultural beliefs, values, traditions, language preferences, and health practices of the communities that we serve and to apply that knowledge to produce positive health outcomes. We also recognize that each of us has a different way of thinking and perceiving our world and that these differences often lead to innovative solutions.

Trinity Health's dedication to diversity includes a unified workforce (through training and education, recruitment, retention and development), commitment and accountability, communication, community partnerships, and supplier diversity.

United States Steel

In order to attract and retain employees with the talents and skills needed for the company to achieve its vision: "Making Steel. World Competitive. Building Value." U. S. Steel is committed to creating an environment that values people's differences.

Established in 2006 and working closely with a Diversity Council made up of employees with different backgrounds, U. S. Steel's Corporate Diversity Department is focused on attracting, training and retaining a world-class workforce. This is essential to sustaining our global operations at a time when the demographics of America are changing and the labor force is growing at a slower pace. The department's immediate goals include training our existing workforce on our new diversity initiatives and recruiting new employees with a variety of educational, work, community service and life experiences for positions throughout the company.

Walmart

We believe that business wins when everyone matters. We remain competitive by leveraging diverse perspectives to drive business solutions; expanding our talent pipeline to create a sustainable company; and demonstrating global cultural competence to better serve our customers, associates, communities and suppliers.

Walmart Office of Diversity Core Objectives:

- To align diversity strategies and goals directly with our business.

- To continue to build a diverse leadership pipeline and workforce.

- To model inclusive leadership through mentoring and outreach to diverse organizations.

- To serve as the leading employer, retailer and neighbor of choice.

- To enhance our relationships with diverse suppliers.

WellPoint, Inc.

Everything we do at WellPoint is focused on our mission of improving the lives of the people we serve and the health of our communities. This spirit drives our commitment to create the best health care value for our customers, while advocating for responsible health care reform in America. It sets the foundation for our success as the nation's largest health benefits company and it strongly influences our approach to diversity as a competitive advantage.

At WellPoint, we are determined to provide quality health care plans to our members and to deliver products and services that anticipate and meet customer needs. We understand that diversity is essential to our success, as we deliver on this commitment by:

- Recruiting and retaining the best talent from ALL walks of life

- Developing products and marketing initiatives that resonate with, and appeal to a diverse consumer base

- Cultivating a culturally competent workforce that understands what drives our consumers' buying decisions, and the needs of the diverse underinsured and uninsured market

- Understanding and communicating that diversity management is not just race, gender, age, sexual orientation or disability, but rather a comprehensive strategy for business success

- We believe in the power of diversity, the role it plays in creating a culture of distinction and the impact it has on improving our member and provider service satisfaction, our associate and consumer engagement and, ultimately, a brighter future.

Case Study:
Marriott International, Inc.

Marriott International's commitment to diversity can be summed up in one word—absolute. To Marriott, diversity is more than a goal, it is a business imperative. Nineteen years after Marriott became the first hospitality company to implement a diversity program, the company still continues to make great strides in the diversity and inclusion world. Initially, the company's initiatives only focused on workplace programs, but today Marriott's D&I focus includes employees, owners, customers, franchisees, and suppliers.

In 2003, the company established its "Committee for Excellence," which meets regularly to set important diversity goals for the company and oversees the progress at every level of the organization. Marriott also has three regional diversity councils that work to make sure that the company's diversity message is translated well throughout its communications, in its recruitment efforts, and in its relationships with other corporations.

Another facet of Marriott's strong commitment to diversity and inclusion can be seen through its diversity ownership program. The company reports that more than 430 of its hotels are owned, operated, or under construction by minorities and women.

Through its supplier diversity program, the company has spent $500 million with multicultural firms and has put forth a goal of spending 15 percent with multicultural firms.

The company's efforts to ensure all of its employees feel included and important extend to employees with disabilities as well. Marriott's hotels work with many community-based disability organizations and high schools to help prepare individuals with disabilities for employment in the hospitality industry. A few years ago, the company introduced its "We Welcome Service Animals" training program, which assists its hotels in helping to make its guests with disabilities who have service animals feel comfortable during their stay. Additionally, more than 10,000 young persons with disabilities have gotten job and life training skills through Marriott's "Bridges…from School to Work" program.

Chapter 5

Diversity & Inclusion Leadership

Contributor: Alignment Strategies, Dr. Vanessa Weaver

A strong corporate culture that invests in diversity and inclusion is one of the greatest competitive advantages a company can maintain. In no area of business has corporate leadership and learning been more essential to progress than in guiding our companies through the culture shift of embracing diversity and inspiring inclusiveness. True leaders must boldly lead their organizations in all facets of business while at the same time be open to learning from their top management, employees, and peers to keep ahead of new ideas and surging events.

In this chapter, we will explore the following questions:

• What are the various phases of diversity and inclusion leadership maturity?

• How does an organization move from a "country-centric" diversity leadership paradigm to a global one?

• What is a typical organizational structure for diversity and inclusion leadership?

• What is the role of the Board of Directors in diversity and inclusion?

• How are best practices companies leveraging diversity councils?

• How important is CEO commitment?

• What are some best practices evidenced by leading CEOs and their companies?

The New Global Leadership Paradigm

The year 2010 marks almost five decades of the exploding genre now known as "Diversity and Inclusion," or D&I. Forerunners to D&I had defining titles, representing "Phases" of diversity maturity such as: EEO, Affirmative Action, Multiculturalism, Diversity, Inclusion, and now, Diversity and Inclusion. Major social movements such as the Civil, Women's, and LGBT Rights movements, influenced the earliest Phases (1960-1980). Legislative mandates, such as the Civil Rights Act, Title I, and Equal Employment Opportunity defined their focus. Since the 1990's, marketplace realities have represented major shifts from "country-centric" to global. The global shift, fueled by rapid changes in technology, made access to global markets and communities just a click, call, or screen away. This "global-centric" focus has created global marketplace interdependence with an urgency to fully capitalize on D&I to drive its value equation. The chart that follows presents Alignment Strategies' Diversity Continuum Stages Maturity Model, which showcases the various Phases of diversity maturity and how this impacts various focus areas in each Phase.

Diversity and Inclusion Continuum

Affirmative Action 1960-1975	Multiculturalism 1975-1985	Diversity and Inclusion 1985 - Present
Based on legal and moral motives	Flows from corporate image and social responsibility	Based on competitive advantage - makes good business sense
Issue: getting numbers in	Issue: keeping numbers in	Issue: moving numbers up/breaking glass ceiling
Strategy: Recruitment	Strategy: training programs	Strategy: systemic interventions
Limited inclusion, mainly Black/White	Broadened to include White women, some ethnic groups	All inclusive - White males, women, people of color, age, ethnic groups, etc.
Grounded in "Be seen but not heard"	Grounded in assimilation and "Melting pot" vision	Grounded in "Tapestry" approach
Assumption minorities and women were getting something for nothing: less qualified	Successful minorities and women viewed as exceptions to rule: still required special treatment	Onus on organization to create environment enabling/encouraging all people to contribute
People who are different need to be "fixed" to fit; deficit model	More "okay" to be different, but onus on minority/woman to fit in	Differences have business benefits; require new management skills to leverage this potential but they have positive impact on all employees
Manage by the numbers: avoid litigation, being cited by the government	Supervisors required to make "it" work on case by case basis	Organization addresses systemic requirements for leveraging differences (testing, career development, evaluations)
Consequences: lose - lose	Consequences: win - lose	Consequences: win - win

The presence of a diverse and inclusive workplace culture is perhaps the greatest business catalyst that exists to tap the potential and profit of emerging markets, broaden the talent pipeline, and enhance brand and corporate reputation. For diversity and inclusion to be successful, however, it must be planted, nurtured, and exposed to the right conditions over time. This joint effort requires the commitment of individuals throughout all levels and locations of an organization, yet strong and genuine leadership is what allows diversity and inclusion to thrive.

Understanding Our Past Leadership Lessons

The benefit of D&I is that it provides us with over 50 years of knowledge regarding D&I leadership in various stages. As we move into the second decade of the 21st century, we have a solid leadership foundation on which to build. Interestingly, organizational leaders in the early stages of diversity maturity during the 1960s to '70s held similar attributes with those who led major social movements.

Similar to Bass' Trait Theory of Leadership Development, many early diversity leaders possessed a passion to right wrongs and injustices that they observed in their organizations. They had personal leadership qualities that enabled them to gain the confidence of their organizations to help navigate this often-difficult terrain but did not have diversity training or the benefit of our 50 years of knowledge.

Other leaders rose out of organizational crises, such as being sued or boycotted for transgressions against legislative mandates, poor corporate branding, or diversity practices that eroded in their ability to compete. Although generations benefited from their sacrifice, these leaders often did not reap the personal career benefits of their contributions and leadership. Like their social movement counterparts, many of their careers were cut short and/or derailed.

Creating the New Paradigm

Fully capitalizing on the value equation for D&I in the 21st century will require leaders who can lead globally complex, culturally diverse, and interrelated organizations. This will require a new cadre of leaders, with vision, experience, and global cultural competencies.

Leadership is a universal, global competence. At its core are basic elements that are present in tribal leaders in small villages in Africa as well as CEOs of Fortune 100 global companies. Leadership is defined as "a process by which a person influences others to accomplish an objective and directs the organization in a way that makes it more cohesive and coherent." Leaders carry out this process by applying their own beliefs, values, ethics, character, knowledge, and skills.

The benefit of developing a global diversity leadership paradigm is the concept of "intentionality" and "choice." In the earlier phases, business was driven to address diversity by a tsunami of social change. As a result, we stumbled onto many of our diversity lessons and figured out how to lead. Now there is recognition of the need to be more deliberate in choosing our D&I leaders who are committed to their skill enhancement. In fact, the current focus on global cultural competency as a requisite for D&I leadership is recognition that we are choosing to learn how to become transformational D&I leaders. This type of diversity leader is capable in any global and cultural context and at any stage of organizational diversity maturity. This leader lives the mantra: "Be, Know, Do." In the context of diversity and inclusion leadership, let us explore this transformational leader mantra:

BE who leaders are—including their beliefs and character.
Leaders share their personal diversity and inclusion beliefs and know how they can drive value for the individual, group, and organization. Leaders demonstrate their character by their willingness to understand and incorporate diverse points of view within a global context. They take personal responsibility for global diversity and inclusion failures and share its successes with their team.

KNOW what leaders know—including job and human skills and knowledge.
Diversity and inclusion leaders invest in developing their individual and team D&I competencies and skill sets. They ensure that there is an understanding of how D&I supports the organization's overall strategy. These leaders help employees or team members link their individual contributions to the success of the diversity and inclusion initiative to the business. They communicate the on-going status of the diversity and inclusion impact and its global implications.

DO what leaders do—in terms of implementing, motivating, and providing direction.
Diversity and inclusion leaders support development of customized goals, values, and concepts that are relevant to global markets, yet have local applications in specific work environments. They clarify roles and responsibilities. These leaders differentiate between the culture and climate. The transformational D&I leader, while acknowledging cultural norms and limitations, leads their team beyond the sometimes confining limitations of culture and restrictive beliefs about climate. These leaders demonstrate personal courage of conviction. They also motivate others to step into their own greatness.

Leadership Structure and Organizational Chart

An effective diversity and inclusion initiative features internal and external leveraging across the organization, throughout the business units, to customers and community. The effective diversity and inclusion office equals leverage and access for the purpose of being a competitive organization. What is important is access at the top including the CEO, Board of Directors, and diversity and inclusion councils and business units.

The Diversity Best Practices organizational chart on the next page demonstrates the following best-practice principles:

- Support from top management

- Diversity and inclusion responsibility in operational functions

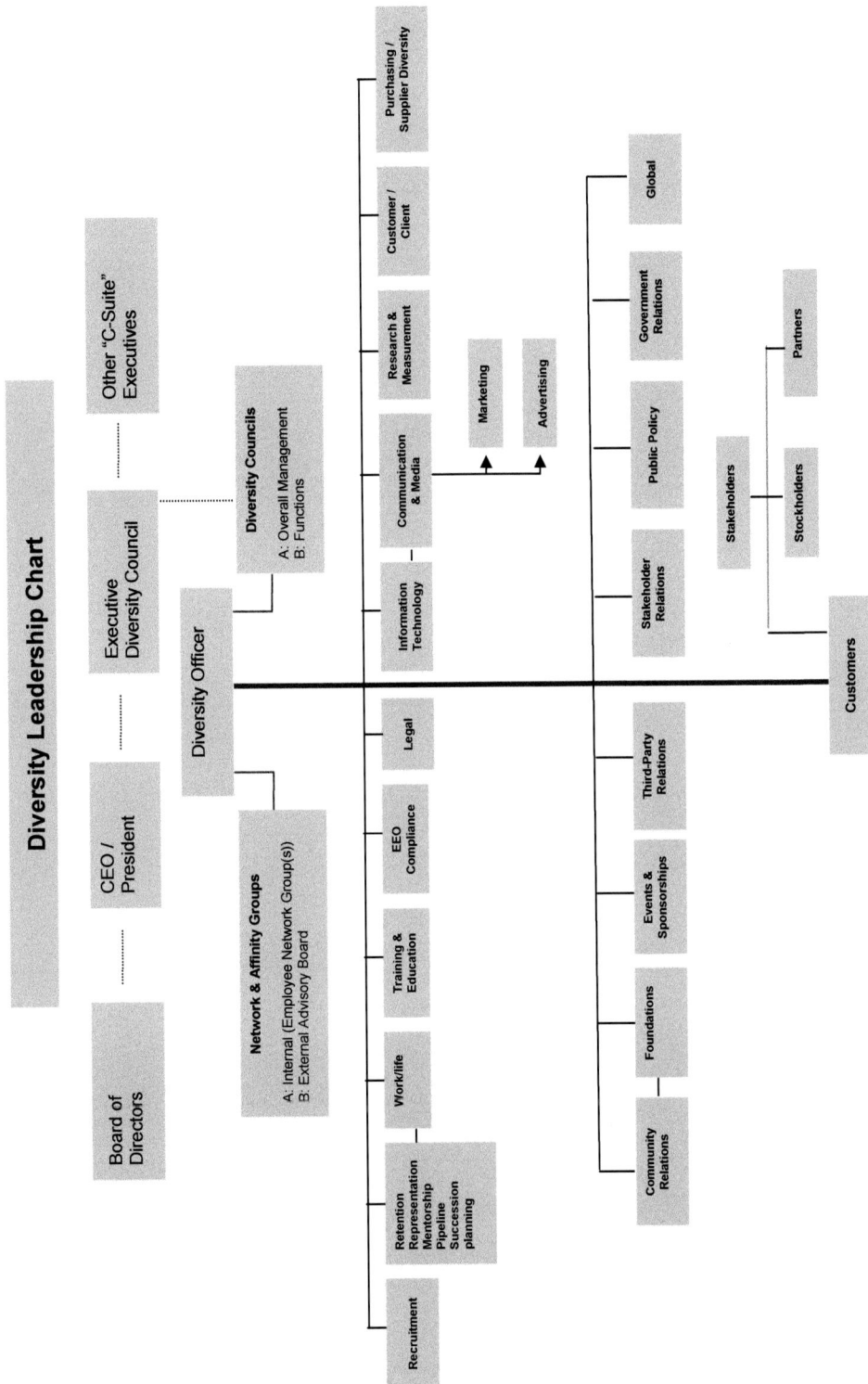

Diversity Leadership Chart

Board of Directors

CEO / President

Executive Diversity Council

Other "C-Suite" Executives

Diversity Officer

Diversity Councils
A: Overall Management
B: Functions

Network & Affinity Groups
A: Internal (Employee Network Group(s))
B: External Advisory Board

Recruitment

Retention
Representation
Mentorship
Pipeline
Succession planning

Work/life

Training & Education

EEO Compliance

Legal

Information Technology

Communication & Media

Research & Measurement

Customer / Client

Purchasing / Supplier Diversity

Marketing

Advertising

Community Relations

Foundations

Events & Sponsorships

Third-Party Relations

Stakeholder Relations

Public Policy

Government Relations

Global

Stakeholders

Stockholders

Partners

Customers

- Demonstration of different functions that make for best-in-class diversity and inclusion

If the functions and responsibilities are aligned, there is greater commitment, efficiency, effectiveness, productivity, and revenue. Alignment is one major aspect of success. The other is the success of each function as it is applied to diversity and inclusion.

Functions and Roles

Diversity and inclusion is only as effective as the functions with which it becomes integrated. For diversity and inclusion to become a strategic business driver, leaders must understand which functions must embrace diversity and inclusion—and then work to implement appropriate synergies.

No company or government agency we are currently aware of claims to have reached the point of total integration of diversity and inclusion initiatives into all of the major business functions listed below. All have more to accomplish in terms of outreach and inclusive strategies. Many companies have developed significant synergies in as many as seven or eight of these functions. For this reason, we believe that integration is evolving and will become a bigger business imperative in the coming years.

Today, diversity and inclusion leadership is being challenged to support the workforce internally and myriad constituencies and communities externally. Leadership is about fitting the pieces of the puzzle together. Diversity and inclusion incorporates the full integration of policies, practices and program initiatives, all measured to ensure accountability. Diversity and inclusion demands building relationships every step of the way.

Best practice diversity and inclusion leaders integrate D&I across companies in the following functions:

- Workforce
  › HR linkages
  › Recruitment and retention
  › Succession planning and pipeline development
  › Matrix measurement of workforce changes
  › Work/life
  › Mentoring, reverse mentoring, sponsorship, networking, and other support systems
  › Internal awards and recognition
  › Other ancillary supportive functions
- EEO and Legal Compliance
- Diversity Councils: executive, business units

- Affinity Groups

- Training and Education

- Supplier Diversity

- Communications

- Advertising

- Multicultural Marketing and Sales

- Third Party Partnerships, External Networking Groups, and Public Policy Outreach

- Stockholder Relations

- Special Events and Sponsorships

- Foundation and Philanthropy

- Government Relations

- Community Relations

At leading companies, diversity and inclusion acts as a bridge between workforce and marketplace, transferring commitment to innovation and inclusion into all arenas in which business is conducted. The intent is to move minorities and women in and up the pipeline. Diversity and inclusion recruiting programs are focused on changing the numbers from entry-level positions to Boardroom seats. The private sector is changing fast with many companies adopting aggressive goals to meet the new demographics. From a business perspective, the highly diverse, multicultural marketplace is one of the most rapidly expanding segments of consumers in this country.

Some key factors to consider when crafting true D&I leadership include:

- **Commitment from CEOs, Boards of Directors, and top management** Top-level commitment to diversity with an inclusive "seat at the table" based on the expressed understanding of the impact diversity and inclusion has on the bottom line. This commitment extends to performance measurement by ensuring that the bonus and reward structure is tied to diversity and inclusion goals and achievement.

- **Diversity and Inclusion Officer** Senior diversity and inclusion officer with key staff support the diversity and inclusion team. Best-in-class companies almost always have a direct reporting line from the most senior diversity and inclusion officer to the CEO.

- **Strategic plan** Most of the best companies use a strategic plan to integrate elements. They set quantitative and qualitative goals.

- **Executive Diversity and Inclusion Council** A diversity and inclusion council that develops, reviews, and measures broad company diversity and inclusion goals and is supported by other diversity and inclusion councils embedded throughout the business becomes the framework for top-level diversity and inclusion champions. This body uses its position and influence to drive change, continually measuring progress throughout the organization and responding accordingly.

- **Integrated organization:** A sound organizational structure operating under a cross-functional model includes recruitment and retention with upward mobility; mentorship; affinity groups; training and education; communications from Internet; support to internal and external programs; external group liaison; sponsorships and events; philanthropy and community support; supplier diversity; strong research capacity; and measurement support.

- **Measurement and benchmarking systems:** "What gets measured gets done" is the phrase most companies are using. Typically at best-in-class organizations, each program is measured.

- **Multicultural marketing and sales:** There is nothing stronger to support the business case than the tie to the customer and support of new customers.

- **Diversity as impetus for the development of new products and services:** This is a major area of growth. Internal employee network groups are being used for marketing and product development and for focus groups. Global teams are doing the same.

- **Community and philanthropy ties:** The definition of community reaches three levels: local, national, and global. Partnerships and sponsorships are of major importance.

- **Supplier diversity:** Keep in mind that while purchasing has the responsibility, the diversity and inclusion office has the leadership.

- **Best-in-class diversity and inclusion leaders track the effectiveness of programs with meticulous analysis, measuring value and return on investment.** They are able to watch the evolution of diversity initiatives and their subsequent impact on all stakeholders, from shareholders to vendors to customers. Just as D&I is the future of America, so it is also a future return on investment for American business.

Board Leadership

D&I initiatives transcend regular corporate functions because the diversity and inclusion officer and his or her team typically feel they are part of their company's greater mission to build the organization and show an impact as the workforce and marketplace change. Thus, they succeed when they get others in operating units to adapt diversity and inclusion for business reasons.

Companies also are looking at Board diversity more broadly in terms of the unique skills, expertise, and perspectives of their directors. This new focus on Board composition stems from an overall trend in the field of corporate governance that emphasizes strong, active Boards with a majority of independent directors. In response to these changing expectations, companies are looking beyond traditional recruitment sources in an effort to find directors who bring a greater variety of knowledge, experiences, and work styles.

The business and investment communities have long debated the legitimacy of the connection between corporate governance practices and financial performance. Nonetheless, it has become increasingly accepted that the corporate objective of maximizing shareholder value requires not only superior competitive performance, but also attention to a variety of governance issues, including Board diversity.

Board Structure

Best practices are evident in eight areas that affect a Board's work:

Representation

Women, minority, and other underrepresented Board members often champion diversity and inclusion, but these days, white men are increasingly relating diversity and inclusion to the business bottom line as well. To that end, Board representation should reflect the myriad of diverse backgrounds, cultures, and experiences of the communities which it serves.

Engagement

Many Boards perform annual reviews of diversity and inclusion; however, best-practice CEOs study diversity and inclusion every quarter. Some top companies also have Board committees on diversity and inclusion, while others have an executive who takes the lead in engaging the Board in diversity and inclusion discussions.

Six Key Areas for Board Leadership and Oversight

- An external diversity advisory board that advises on corporate governance
- An internal diversity executive council
- A chief diversity officer who reports to a top executive and to the Board
- Guiding principles of diversity and governance
- Bonus systems that include compensation for results
- Board training on D&I

Many Boards are also asking for, and participating in, Board diversity training. Additionally, Board members review upward mobility and pipeline development, sales and multicultural marketplace data, and supplier diversity goals and achievements.

Xerox's Board, for instance, has an annual diversity and inclusion discussion in which Board members discuss how D&I can be part of the company's business strategy. These Board members recognize that D&I discussions are about more than information sharing; they are about improving the company's bottom line.

Simply put, when a Board tracks diversity and inclusion performance, the corporation falls in line. When a Board does not track performance, D&I does not become a priority. Actual numbers on retention, recruitment, etc., can help the Board assess the company's progress.

Diversifying Corporate Boards

Over the last decade, the issue of diversity in the workplace has become a topic of considerable interest and attention in the media, with stakeholders, and for companies. During this time, companies have undertaken a variety of actions and implemented a broad range of programs aimed at hiring, training, and retaining a diverse workforce. More recently, this emphasis on diversity has come to include the issue of Board diversity, as companies are increasingly being called upon to demonstrate an organizational commitment to diversity at the very highest levels of the organization.

Greater Board Diversity

While the representation of women and minorities on corporate Boards continues to lag far behind their numbers among the population at large and barriers to advancement continue to exist, Boards of Directors are slowly shifting in composition to reflect greater racial and gender diversity.

Investor Activism

Board diversity has emerged as a central issue among institutional and activist investors, and shareholder proposals calling for companies to increase and report on their Board diversity have become common.

Stakeholder Activism

A variety of external organizations representing the interests of groups have begun to conduct research and engage in advocacy on the issue of Board diversity. Activities by these groups include conducting annual surveys on the numbers of underrepresented individuals on Boards, rating and ranking companies based on the composition of their Boards, and launching public campaigns asking companies to add women or minority members to their Boards.

Changing Expectations for Corporate Directors

In the last decade, institutional and activist investors have initiated a corporate governance reform movement that has called into question many of the long-standing practices of corporate Boards. Directors are increasingly expected to be independent of management, be active participants, and bring strategically advantageous skills and experiences. At the same time, many companies are limiting the number of outside Boards on which their top executives can serve. As a result, companies are casting a wider net searching outside traditional networks for candidates and contributing to the increases in diversity among corporate directors.

CEO Engagement

CEOs have never been more enthusiastic about diversity and inclusion. Indeed, CEOs recruit most top D&I officers and most, with the support of their Boards, have tied compensation incentives to D&I goals.

Leading CEOs understand that good diversity and inclusion programs boost business. They see that too many D&I efforts have been haphazard—so they ask for integration across business units to ensure a return on investment. When D&I officers report quarterly to the CEO and at least annually to the Board, the whole company hears the message that D&I matters.

In best-practice companies, the CEO has also become the biggest champion of diversity and inclusion programs. These CEOs understand that D&I is an operational issue for the workforce and marketplace. Diversity and inclusion programs can increase productivity and profitability. Diversity and inclusion is not just a community relations necessity—it's a business imperative.

CEO Commitment Is Key

If a CEO chairs the diversity council or meets with it regularly, that company's diversity and inclusion program earns respect and functional integration becomes much easier. Indeed, if the CEO reviews D&I representation goals and performance, the road to success is more certain.

Consider these questions when judging your CEO's commitment:

- Does your workforce understand your CEO's position on diversity and inclusion programs? Do your stakeholders and customers?

- Is your CEO's diversity statement clear and used in your diversity and inclusion materials and on your Internet and Intranet site?

- Are you placing speeches and articles with your communications department that highlight your CEO's diversity and inclusion stance?

- What can you do now to gain more CEO support for diversity and inclusion programs and communicate that support to stakeholders?

Diversity Councils

Examples of Diversity Councils Types

- Executive Council: Generally appointed by the CEO, members of the "C-Suite" and operating companies, this council's function is exemplary of cross-functional representation when done well. The operating level of the diversity council is responsible for the day-to-day oversight of the diversity program.

- Leadership Council: Members are those with functional responsibility who can impact diversity directly.

- Diversity Council: Consists of mid-level representation.

- Operating Company or Division Councils

- Affinity Groups or Networks

- Diversity councils translate the priorities of the steering committee (as applicable) into the realities of the business units. Committee priorities include:

  - Supporting business leaders to solve problems associated with incorporating diversity into day-to-day management practices

  - Collaborating with recruiters and managers to develop and implement effective strategies for hiring and retaining a diverse workforce

  - Sponsoring research to ensure that products/services are developed and marketed to effectively satisfy the interests of a diverse customer base

  - Leading the educational campaign for zero-tolerance for harassment, discrimination, and exclusion.

Diversity Council Leadership

A diversity council leader does not have to be the senior ranking member of the committee but should demonstrate the capacity to focus on the whole enterprise—what is needed and how to make it happen. It is important for the leader to have a track record of consistent high-level job performance over time. He or she should be known (across levels and diverse groups) for objectivity, fairness, and basic good judgment. The diversity leader needs to have authority and decision-making ability as he or she works with the members of the council.

Structure of the Executive Level Diversity Council

A council reports to the CEO, COO, or steering committee and may even include a Board of Directors representative(s). A council is established for an indefinite period of time, supporting business units to internalize diversity and inclusion into the culture of the company.

An increasing number of companies are forming advisory diversity councils made up of outside leaders. In order to achieve its mandate, the council needs clarity, purpose, and accountability. The members can make a concerted effort to play an important role in the diversity program and oversee a diversity and inclusion plan. This works if the members of the council have different backgrounds and perspectives and are committed to diversity and inclusion as a business imperative.

Diversity Council Executive Support/Funding

The business unit head provides its council member(s) with sponsorship, resources, time, and on-going interaction. The council sets concrete annual objectives, and the business unit provides the budget to produce those deliverables. The council and its members are to be held accountable for meeting objectives as any other task force or committee would. (The same process and funding are evidenced as councils are driven into the framework of the company.)

Communications and Visibility

Communications and visibility are important for the council and its members to ensure that all know the governance commitment to diversity. Companies should consider launching of an internal campaign to announce the council's business objectives. Communications to the management and employees will "raise the level of organizational consciousness" such that it develops and maintains an expectation of inclusion and quality treatment for all.

Membership

Representatives from each business unit should serve on the council so that its membership represents a diverse slice of the organization. A percentage of the council should rotate each year, with members expected to serve in the capacity of role models for inclusion.

Setting Standards

Regular attendance at meetings and should be established as criteria for membership on the council and reviewed with the team members.

Each company differs in framework and practices but all must set the right leadership and infrastructure for their organization. They must each set principles, practices, and accountability measures and determine the frequency of meetings by the nature of the objectives to be met. Diversity Best Practices advocates that the mission, vision, operating standards, and procedures be clear, compelling and command accountability.

Creating a Corporate Diversity Steering Committee

The mission and/or objectives of the diversity steering committee are to provide executive leadership and direction to the diversity and inclusion initiative, especially in its early stages. This includes:

- Clearly articulating why inclusion is critical to business success

- Integrating D&I into the business strategy and goals, and communicating those throughout the company

- Aligning human resource policies and management practices with those strategies

- Creating/supporting (as appropriate) other D&I structures (e.g. diversity council, affinity groups, etc.).

Frequency of Meetings

A council typically meets monthly or quarterly at the executive level. Councils meet monthly at the local diversity council level. There may be committees within the diversity council, or members are assigned tasks. Frequency of meetings varies by company and nature of management, with the practices and policies are reviewed with each member.

Still, as governors of diversity and inclusion, the matrix systems, measurements, and framework on achievements are reviewed on a periodic basis. Goals and successes are now most often presented at least annually to the Board of Directors or a committee of the Board.

Conclusion

In this chapter, we:

• Studied the various phases of diversity and inclusion leadership maturity.

• Examined how best practices companies move from a "county-centric" diversity leadership paradigm to a global one.

• Reviewed a typical organizational structure for diversity and inclusion leadership.

• Considered the role of the Board of Directors in diversity and inclusion.

• Investigated how best practices companies are leveraging diversity councils.

• Reiterated the importance of CEO commitment.

• Shared best practices of leading CEOs and their companies.

Diversity and inclusion is a crucial component of any successful and growth-oriented business strategy. True D&I leaders know that a strong diversity and inclusion strategy is vital to bottom-line success, and they deeply understand the business case for building a workforce that is reflective of the ever-changing demographics of the market and the opportunities afforded with diversity as a competitive advantage.

Corporate luminaries of diversity and inclusion demonstrate exemplary leadership as well as innovative and positive responses to demographic shifts in the global workforce and marketplace. These individuals share a tireless commitment and passion for diversity and inclusion within their respective companies. And their experiences prove that diversity isn't just the right thing to do, it is the business thing to do.

Case Study: Dell, Inc.

In today's complex world, many companies are undergoing significant transformations. This is coupled with significant demographic shifts happening in every corner of the world.

Did you know?

- For every one baby born in the U.S.,10 are born in China and India.

- In the U.S., people of color are becoming the majority.

- The next generation of our workforce is driven by values and a desire for work-life balance.

- The majority of small businesses are created and led by women.

These shifts create a time of incredible change and opportunity. This is true for Dell. However, during this time, it is important to understand that Dell is not losing an important foundation for success—its commitment to diversity and inclusion.

The company's diversity and inclusion strategy is simple—helping Dell succeed with a global workforce that is highly talented, committed, and reflective of its global customers. This means that Dell provides an open and inclusive workplace. Dell's definition of diversity covers not only differences in race, gender, and sexual-orientation, but also geographic location, education, work styles, ethnicity, and communications style, among others. Diversity and inclusion are a competitive business advantage.

"We can better serve diverse global customers when we leverage the full benefit of our collective experiences, insights, and talents of our global workforce at all levels of the organization," believes Gil Casellas, vice president, corporate responsibility, and chief diversity officer. "We strive to ensure that each employee is heard and valued and that personal strengths and perspectives are assets to the company, rather than left at the door."

"I'm sometimes asked if diversity is really important to our leadership," continues Casellas. "I can definitely say 'yes.' In fact, diversity and inclusion are a business imperative, opportunity, and responsibility, and it starts at the top. Michael Dell, our chief executive officer chairs our global diversity council, and six executives, three from Dell's Executive Leadership Team, also sit on the council."

The Global Diversity Council has taken an active role in shaping Dell's diversity and inclusion strategy, which will be focused on:

- Strong, visible leadership commitment and clear expectations on accountability for diversity and inclusion

- Genuine commitment to diversity and inclusion built into Dell's business practices

- Thorough integration of these behaviors in Dell's talent and performance management

By providing accountability, priorities, and leadership engagement, the Global Diversity Council and Michael Dell committed to having each member of the executive leadership team (ELT) be accountable for owning their diversity goals and metrics and for prioritizing the retention, recruitment, and development of underrepresented groups in the company's leadership ranks.

Dell's organizational and human resource planning process (OHRP) provides a clear example that diversity is a business priority and that its leadership is committed to making it a reality. In each ELT member's OHRP process with Michael Dell, the diversity and inclusion questions are usually raised by Michael Dell and the individual ELT members, rather than by the chief diversity officer. Says Casellas, "It is reassuring to know that for our CEO, diversity remains a priority even during such tough economic times."

The Dell leadership is becoming more and more engaged in the company's diversity and inclusion efforts. Numerous senior leaders serve on the boards of employee resource groups, and Michael Dell has personally hosted events for high potential diverse employees, met with the executive leadership of employee networking groups, and served as a keynote speaker for an employee resource group meeting to share his personal commitment and vision for diversity and inclusion.

As Dell continues its transformation, diversity and inclusion will remain an integral part of its overall business strategy. By continuing to drive these initiatives throughout the company, Dell hopes to harness each individual's full potential, provide the best Customer Experience, drive innovation, become a better place to work, and ensure it has an inspired workforce.

Case Study:
Sodexo USA, Inc.

Sodexo's commitment and focus to diversity and inclusion within its organization includes a comprehensive, top-down/bottom-up strategy, according to Dr. Rohini Anand, senior vice president and global chief diversity officer. This may seem contradictory, but it is a strategy that has achieved massive success within the company. The inclusive attitude begins at the top, with Anand and CEO Michel Landel. Diversity is one of the six imperatives on Sodexo's national agenda, and diversity leadership is vital for setting the tone and keeping the focus among the company's 125,000 employees.

The benefits of diversity leadership begin with tangible effects on business. "Our senior executives recognize the value diversity brings to business growth," says Landel. "Since we are committed to investing in diversity, we are reaping the results in terms of building alliances with clients who have similar value systems to ours." On more than one occasion, clients have chosen Sodexo based on its diverse environment. This reinforces the importance of diversity among chief executives who then relay that message to their subordinates.

Communication and accountability are the driving forces behind Sodexo's diversity leadership. The CDO herself reports directly to the CEO and is also a member of the executive team which oversees diversity initiatives. The CEO also chairs the Diversity Leadership Council, a group that sets the direction of the company's strategy. Sodexo utilizes e-mails, presentations, meetings, and newsletters to support the message of inclusion among all employees.

Furthermore, Sodexo recently created three Senior Director of Diversity positions within each of the market segments (education, corporate, and health care) that report directly into the market president. This fosters communication and encourages accountability. But perhaps the most innovative strategy is also the most effective. Ten to 15 percent of managers' bonuses and 25 percent of executive team members' bonuses are directly impacted by success in the diversity area. These incentives are given to the deserving regardless of the overall financial performance of the company.

The Diversity Leadership Council is led directly by Landel, for whom diversity is a personal goal. In addition to the CDO and the Senior Directors of Diversity, Sodexo's Office of Diversity includes Executive Team members who play a key role in leading the diversity efforts, with many members actively engaging in community service and receiving external recognition for contributions. Each market segment has a diversity council that helps to drive diversity and inclusion within their respective market segments. The Diversity Leadership Council meets quarterly but reviews progress and results monthly.

This organization has enjoyed many successes, with one of the biggest being, according to its website, that "80 percent of Sodexo's managers firmly believe the company values diversity and inclusion and that its managerial teams are clearly demonstrating this to employees." All of the company's managers, more that 15,000 in total, have completed training in equal employment and affirmative action. Many employees have also gone through awareness and cross-cultural communication training sessions and learning labs. The Diversity Leadership Council has also introduced a diversity scorecard that contains quantitative measurements to help managers and executives judge the success of initiatives and determine incentives.

"I believe that leadership commitment and buy-in is a foundational prerequisite," asserts Anand. "At Sodexo, we have invested considerable time and resources in ensuring that we have the executive buy-in necessary for any culture change initiative."

Chapter 6

Diversity and Inclusion Officers

The importance of the Chief Diversity and Inclusion Officer roles and the diversity and inclusion office is growing. The functional office of diversity and inclusion has been elevated to the "C-Suite" within most companies today, and diversity and inclusion officer functions have grown over the course of the past five years and are expected to be elevated even further as the need for dynamic competencies has broadened and the impact and scope of these officers has expanded.

For today's diversity and inclusion officer, leadership and business acumen are fundamental to success. Whether the officer is elevated internally or hired from outside, the job is demanding. It requires access at the top and competency to be a change agent. The job of the diversity and inclusion officer also requires more than a desire to impact the workforce at all levels. Most senior diversity and inclusion officers are involved in setting business goals. Diversity and inclusion is critical to the accomplishment of goals and, if used appropriately, to surpass competition.

The diversity and inclusion officer should be strategic in nature. This officer is the personification of the company's identity as an employer of choice. The diversity and inclusion officer also provides important linkages with other functional areas such as marketing, legal, and HR. It requires leadership, judgment, management, mentorship, and results-orientation. D&I officers are leaders by example who empower stakeholders without micromanaging them.

In this chapter, we will explore the following questions:

• What are the typical competencies and responsibilities of a diversity and inclusion officer?

• To whom does the diversity and inclusion officer usually report?

• What are the typical title, compensation, and career length of a diversity and inclusion officer?

•What type of interaction does the diversity and inclusion officer have with the CEO and Board of Directors?

• How has globalization affected the role of the diversity and inclusion officer?

Reporting and Structure

Today, diversity and inclusion officers are reporting at a higher level than ever before. Many are reporting directly to CEOs, presidents, or EVPs rather than being situated further down the leadership chain under the HR umbrella. Even if it is not a direct report, we still see the influence and involvement of those at the top.

No matter the report, the most successful diversity and inclusion leaders report on the progress of initiatives to the corporate board of directors and top management. They do this on a regular basis, generally through the Executive Diversity and Inclusion Council.

Diversity and Inclusion Officer Competencies

Diversity and inclusion officer competencies have dramatically expanded. Successful diversity and inclusion officers must be change agents with business acumen. The capacity to influence and impact an organization and to be a catalyst and a strategist is emphasized by most companies deemed successful.

Diversity Best Practices surveyed leading diversity and inclusion officers, asking them to rate their strength throughout several key competency areas. The following chart highlights the results:

Competency	Index Score
Leadership	9.615
Influence with executive suite	9.487
Support of CEO or top others	9.461
Driving changes	9.333
Focusing on results	9.231
Building trust and integrity	9.077
Building strategic partnerships	8.897
Building and maintaining relationships	8.872
Communications skills	8.743
Business Acumen	8.667
Organizational awareness	8.513
Cross cultural sensitivity	8.205
Global experience	6.62

The survey also found that the average corporate D&I officer:

- has spent 10 years in his or her company

- views the role as a career if responsibility is broad and the diversity and inclusion executive's function is more universal (not HR restricted)

- holds the position anywhere from 1 to 16 years

The diversity and inclusion officer post is increasingly seen as a career. Overall, diversity and inclusion officers who take a great deal of pride in their work are seen as change agents. When given access to and championed by the "C-Suite," many executives have found this to be a rewarding career.

Diversity and Inclusion Officer Compensation

A Diversity Best Practices survey of more than 150 diversity and inclusion officers found the average diversity and inclusion officer salary to be approximately $225,000, comparable to average C-Suite salaries. (Among more than 150 diversity and inclusion officers surveyed, more than 40 earned more than $300,000 per year (base and bonus).

Senior Diversity and Inclusion Officer Compensation Level	Percentage of survey responses
Salary base $300,000+, with a bonus in the range of $100,000	23.3%
Salary base $200,000 - 300,000, with a bonus in the $75,0000 range	46.4%
Salary base $100,000 - 200,000, with a bonus in the $50,000 range	30.3%

Diversity and Inclusion Officer Titles

Diversity and inclusion officer titles are tied to authority and responsibility. There has been an increase in recent years in the naming of diversity and inclusion officers at the senior level.

A Diversity Best Practices survey of D&I officers found that 34.7 percent of companies bestowed the position of diversity and inclusion officer with a title of senior vice president or above.

The most common titles included:

- Vice President – 64.7%

- Chief Diversity Officer – 23.5%

- Director – 17.1%

- Senior Vice President – 8.8%

Functional Responsibilities

Diversity and inclusion officer functions are becoming ever more expansive. Indeed, the word *integration* is understood clearly by effective diversity and inclusion offices. Functional requirements of diversity and inclusion officers include:

- Strong Leadership

- Business Acumen

- Good Judgment

- Effective Management

- Active Mentorship

- Results Orientation

- Short- and Long-Term Visionary

- Team-Oriented

The diversity and inclusion officer role throughout best-practice companies cuts across functions ranging from strategic roles and business planning both in the United States and globally, to include recruiting and retention, pipeline development, compliance, markets, communications, external relations and partnerships, events and sponsorships, global diversity and inclusion, and supplier diversity. The best diversity and inclusion officers are aligned with senior management as they are involved in enhancing business performance.

The senior diversity and inclusion officer understands how and why functional integration is so important to demonstrating the value of the diversity and inclusion function. Many of the senior diversity and inclusion officers have previously worked in HR on recruiting and retention. Many have placed a strong emphasis on work/life functions, especially when retention measurement is a major component of the diversity and inclusion portfolio. Some have legal backgrounds with experience in EEO law and compliance.

The senior diversity and inclusion officer has responsibility beyond HR and the workforce, however. The senior diversity and inclusion officer brings credibility to, and an understanding of, the functions reviewed here, including market share, marketing, communications, culture and business growth.

The responsibilities of the senior diversity and inclusion officer are significant, if diversity and inclusion is included in business plans and programs. The skill set for the diversity and inclusion leader is for an intelligent, visionary, results-driven individual—a team player who serves as advisor, change agent and manager of results. Those best positioned for success are those who report to the top and command respect from the CEO and the Board of Directors.

By contrast, diversity and inclusion programs that report through HR still may succeed but won't have the force of an integrated program or the influence necessary to have maximum impact throughout the various lines of business.

Responsibilities of diversity and inclusion officers may include:

- Counselor and advisor

- Business strategist

- Staffing support at all levels

- Workforce development and succession planning

- Creation of diverse talent both at headquarters and in the business units

- Training and education

- Compliance

- Policies, especially as they apply to women and a diverse and inclusive workforce, work/life, and leadership

- Recruiting

- Innovation

- Diversity Council and affinity group relations

- Marketing and marketplace development

- Communications

- Sponsorships

- Partnerships

- Community and philanthropy

- Supplier diversity and inclusion

- Global business

- Ethics

- Government contracting

- Other issues (e.g. labor relationships to safety to the environment)

CEO and Board Involvement

Leadership of the diversity and inclusion officer and executives is deeply connected. Effective CEOs and top officers review, participate in, and ensure that compensation of top executives and managers is linked to success against diversity and inclusion goals.

The value of the diversity and inclusion officer is recognized by leading CEOs and Boards of Directors. Diversity Best Practices reviews indicate that out of 100 D&I officers surveyed, at least 75% report to the board on a regular basis.

Frequency of Board and Diversity and Inclusion Officer Meetings:

- Reporting once per year: 30%

- Reporting every six months: 18%

- Reporting every quarter on some issue: 26%

- Reporting periodically: 13%

- Reporting on some things quarterly and major presentation annually: 8%

When it comes to board engagement, the focus is on who tracks performance. When a board tracks performance, its corporation gets in line. When a board does not track performance, diversity and inclusion performance typically falls far to the bottom of the priority list.

Eight Areas Reflecting Board Leadership and Oversight:

- Representation

- Engagement

- External diversity and inclusion advisory board

- Internal diversity and inclusion executive council

- Chief diversity and inclusion officer

- Guiding principles and governance

- Bonus system

- Board training for diversity and inclusion

Globalization and the Role of the Diversity and Inclusion Officer

Globalization is reshaping the responsibilities as it deeply impacts business strategies. The diversity and inclusion function will play an increasingly significant role in the support of globalization efforts. Some core global issues facing diversity and inclusion officers include:

- Setting corporate-wide diversity and inclusion policies that are consistent worldwide

- Navigating the legal obstacles of implementing diversity and inclusion initiatives throughout different countries

- Allocating the right staff and budget while building a talent pool within different cultures that will garner business results and community support

- Using a mix of local diversity and inclusion councils and employee resource groups

- Developing the right tools, techniques, and training programs

- Building the base for communications and marketing support programs utilizing goals and solid measurements

- Ensuring that diversity and inclusion awareness training classes are tailored for the business case in each country

- Translating domestic diversity and inclusion programs for use globally and learning from global initiatives to enhance and strengthen the U.S. program

- Building community support

- Tying the program to philanthropy support

- Nurturing governmental ties with the local community to enhance global diversity and inclusion efforts

- Measuring programs to ensure accountability

- Reviewing the tracking system and ROI and adapting as warranted

Conclusion

In this chapter, we:

- Discussed the typical competencies and responsibilities of a diversity and inclusion officer.

- Analyzed the reporting structure of the diversity and inclusion officer.

- Noted the typical title, compensation, and career length of a diversity and inclusion officer.

- Examined the type of interaction the diversity and inclusion officer has with the CEO and Board of Directors.

- Investigated the effect of globalization on the role of the diversity and inclusion officer.

Diversity and inclusion officers are charged with helping to create an atmosphere where all people feel welcome and valued. To that end, the challenge of today's diversity and inclusion officer is to ensure that employees of all backgrounds and beliefs are able to come together for the common purpose of seeing the company succeed nationally and globally. Additionally, the diversity and inclusion officer is essential in helping to position the company's products and services as number one in the eyes of consumers.

Business growth results from diversity and inclusion and innovation sets best companies apart from their competition. If diversity and inclusion is the vehicle by which many companies are attempting to reach and surpass their workplace and marketplace goals, then the diversity and inclusion officer is at the helm.

Chapter 7

Budget and Staffing

Thus far, we have clearly established the business case for diversity and inclusion. Diversity and inclusion helps position a company as an employer of choice, and therefore, supports the recruiting and retention functions. Diversity and inclusion also helps to promote a company as a supplier of choice for goods and services to an ever-evolving consumer base. However, in order to support numerous functions companywide and aid the organization in revenue generation, the diversity and inclusion office must first have adequate resources, including a budget and staff that are large enough to allow it to perform its functions fully and at top quality.

At some companies, D&I is housed under Human Resources; at others, the D&I function has its own office and a Chief Diversity Officer who reports directly to the CEO. Given these variables, budgets and staffing for D&I vary widely across industries and regions and also depend on the responsibilities that fall within the function at large. Most importantly, companies must assess D&I responsibilities and desired outcomes for their own unique organization and determine appropriate budget and staffing needs from there.

In this chapter, we will explore the following questions:

- What functions and roles does the diversity and inclusion budget usually cover?

- On average, how much do diversity and inclusion officers get paid?

- How do diversity and inclusion budgets vary across industries?

- What functions and positions are typically found within the diversity and inclusion office?

Setting Goals and Objectives

When evaluating and funding a corporate diversity and inclusion initiative, companies need to look at the business case for diversity in that corporate environment. There are countless reasons for creating a culture of inclusion. Business leaders at companies with established workplace D&I programs need to support such initiatives by communicating them as top priorities to employees, customers, and the business community and by funding diversity and inclusion recruitment and retention initiatives.

There are far too many variables company-by-company and industry-by-industry for averages to be useful. There are no easy answers in terms of budgeting and staffing because functional definitions differ as to where to place the budgets. What is important is to tackle each of the functions and share information on functions that are increasing, staying the same, and decreasing—and why.

Diversity and inclusion initiatives differ greatly in companies based on different goals and objectives. However, all of the following initiatives can greatly impact the D&I office's budget:

- Business development activities

- Holidays, celebrations, and culture-ties

- Customer base and new markets

- Internal and external linkages to networks and organizations

- Communications

- Community relations and philanthropy (e.g. events and sponsorships)

- Supplier diversity

A recent study released by the Society of Human Resource Management (SHRM) reported diversity-department budgets at Fortune 1000 companies average around $1.5 million per year. The range for diversity department budgets was $30,000 to $5.1 million. When diversity was housed in Human Resources, the average annual diversity budget was $239,000.

Some of these budgets may include multicultural marketing and advertising; however, many companies report those expenditures under marketing or sales while advertising funds for D&I are typically reported with the advertising budgets. The philanthropy and community relations budgets are reported under separate areas, but again, comprise a key component in the best companies. Diversity and inclusion education, training, and e-learning are generally the largest upfront costs. At times they are allocated to diversity and inclusion, but more often they are allocated to the overall HR training budget since training and development can be investments that are tied to so many areas and at so many levels.

Workforce Management estimates that companies spend a combined $8 billion on diversity and inclusion training annually, while *Human Resource Management Journal* reports that diversity and inclusion consultants earn a combined $400 million to $600 million annually in consulting fees alone.

Budget Distribution

The budget equation involves many variables, including:

- Areas within functions

- Where training budgets lie

- How much of the communications and advertising for diversity and inclusion might be tied to the diversity and inclusion budget

- Whether the EEO and compliance function is under diversity and inclusion; the same is true for the ethics function and even more for multicultural marketing

- Whether they include significant funds for organization support

- Network group funding

Catalyst reports that 82 percent of its member companies have a specific budget for diversity programs and activities. These budgets range broadly from $10,000 to $216 million, with a median budget of $1.2 million. Almost half of the respondents reported allocating the greatest percentage of their overall diversity budget to diversity and inclusion training programs and general administrative costs.

Directing diversity funds for outreach and/or recruiting (45 percent) was also a large portion of the budget. Thirty-nine percent of respondents reported that more than 25 percent of their diversity budget went towards general administrative costs and 25 percent of respondents reported that diversity marketing accounts for more than 25 percent of their budget. Work/life programs and supplier diversity received the lowest levels of budget allocation, with nearly one-half (47 percent) allocating less than 10 percent to each. As is expected, industry type was a large factor in the varying allocations.

Definitions of what is a direct-cost allocation to the diversity budget versus indirect or allocated to another unit in the company, staff or business unit varies. Note that the functional areas of diversity and inclusion are often tied in many ways to company budgeting systems.

Diversity and Inclusion Staffing

The salaries of diversity and inclusion staff members are usually directly attributed to the overall budget, or, in certain instances, companies use dotted-line budget shares. There are the headquarters' staff budgets and then those of diversity and inclusion officers out in the business units.

Staffing components may include:

- Recruiting

- Retention staff functions with mentoring and other tools to support the function; pipeline and succession planning

- Affinity and network groups and support for diversity and inclusion council(s)

- EEO, Affirmative Action and compliance

- Legal costs for diversity and inclusion

- Diversity initiatives/programs

- Diversity communications

- Technology (generally recorded as a corporate overhead expense)

- Sales and multicultural marketing

- Events and sponsorships

- Third-party relationships

- Public policy and government relationships

- Foundations and philanthropy

- Global diversity and inclusion staffing

- Community relations

- Ethics training and compliance

- Supplier diversity (most companies have under procurement with trend moving under chief diversity officer as well)

While diversity and inclusion budgets have taken a hit in recent years, over the long term budgets have been increasing, with the staffing allocated to support business units also on the rise. Going forward, as the economy improves, we see greater accountability as well as increasing support and elevation of the function, the staff, and the resources necessary to build the multicultural workforce, market, and supplier base.

Conclusion

In this chapter, we:

- Explored the functions and roles typically covered by the diversity and inclusion budget.

- Discussed the average compensation for a diversity and inclusion officer.

- Examined the functions and positions that are typically found within the diversity and inclusion office.

Despite cuts in budget and staffing as a result of recent economic challenges, over the long term, budgets and staffing for diversity and inclusion are increasing. There is increasing support and accountability of the diversity and inclusion function, staff, and resources necessary to build the multicultural workforce, customer base, and supplier pool. This is good news given that the D&I function encompasses many roles and responsibilities, and these roles and responsibilities will only grow in extent in the future.

Top corporations and the CEOs that lead them have come to know first hand the power of diversity and inclusion to their bottom line. If they want to continue to realize the benefits that D&I brings to the company, they must provide adequate resources for D&I budgets and staffing.

Chapter 8

Recruitment, Retention, and Advancement

Winning the race for diverse talent requires successful recruiting strategies and savvy retention and talent development tactics. Today's global marketplace is in a state of constant evolution—an ever-changing environment that demands corporate entities keep up with the pace of transformation. Women and the traditional ethnic markets of African Americans, Asian Americans, Hispanics, and Native Americans are now further segmented into other sub-markets such as the lesbian, gay, bisexual, and transgender (LGBT) community, people with disabilities, older Americans, immigrants, and more.

With this major change across the marketplace comes the need to alter the makeup of the corporate workforce. In order to maintain a hold on traditional markets, while also gaining market share in the emerging areas, U.S. companies are finding innovative ways to diversify their workforces to match these consumer bases. Moreover, it is not just about recruiting diverse employees, it is about retaining and developing their professional talents as well.

In this chapter, we will explore the following questions:

- What is the representation of minorities and women in the United States?

- How do best practices companies recruit and retain minorities and women?

- What are key ways to retain and develop women of color specifically?

- Why do employees, particularly minorities and women, leave or stay?

- What impact can mentoring have on recruitment, retention, and advancement?

- What are the current trends in career development and succession planning?

Key Population Trends

Even a quick glance at population statistics will show the importance of staying ahead of the recruitment and retention curve. For example, consider age trends. With four generations now in the workforce, companies looking to lead in the coming decades will have to implement strategies to continually develop their experienced older workers while at the same time compete effectively for younger workers. Additionally, creating synergy between these generational groups—many of whom have differing values, experiences, and work habits—will be a necessity to maintain maximum productivity and a competitive edge.

The changes in the country's population landscape do not end with age. When examining population changes by race and ethnicity, distinct patterns also emerge. For example, based on U.S. Census projections:

- The nation's Hispanic and Asian populations will triple over the next half century, and non-Hispanic whites will represent about one-half of the total population by 2050.

- Nearly 67 million people of Hispanic origin (of any race) will be added to the nation's population between 2000 and 2050. Their numbers are projected to grow from 35.6 million to 102.6 million, an increase of 188 percent. Their share of the nation's population would nearly double, from 12.6 percent to 24.4 percent.

- The nation's Hispanic and Asian populations will triple over the next half century, and non-Hispanic whites will represent about one-half of the total population by 2050.

- The Black population is projected to rise from 35.8 million to 61.4 million in 2050, an increase of about 26 million, or 71 percent. All told, their share of the country's population is expected to increase to 14.6 percent from 12.7 percent.

In addition to the trends in populations by age as well as race and ethnicity, the female population is also projected to continue to outnumber the male population, going from a difference of 5.3 million in 2000 (143.7 million females and 138.4 million males) to 6.9 million (213.4 million females and 206.5 million males) by 2050, according to U.S. Census figures.

With the face of the global workforce changing drastically, it becomes increasingly apparent that winning the race for diverse talent necessitates more than simply adhering to baseline Equal Employment Opportunity and legal requirements. In today's marketplace, best-practice companies are those that integrate diversity philosophy into their business missions.

Recruitment and Retention of Minorities and Women

Diversity sits at the heart of new, innovative, and effective corporate recruiting strategies. The high-stakes global race for talent is precisely why there is more attention on recruiting than ever. Leading corporations say that great recruiting makes the difference in a competitive marketplace and in pushing stock value.

To find qualified minority candidates, the industry is reaching out to students as early as junior high with internships and communications programs. Companies are also seeking candidates from academic areas outside of the company's focus to find those with backgrounds that could be valuable. In addition to networking, they are advertising in minority media outlets, pushing recruiters to find more minority candidates, and sending more staffers to job fairs sponsored by minority organizations.

Inclusive and growth-oriented recruiting must also ensure that the best and brightest female and minority candidates stay with the company once presented with career options. From an economic standpoint, when employees leave and replacements are hired, companies must deal with higher recruiting costs, longer training time, and lower productivity. Research suggests that the cost of a professional or a manager leaving an organization can be as high as twice the average associate's salary or a minimum of one year's worth of salary and benefits. A diverse workforce also inherently brings to the table a diversity of thought and perspective that is extremely valuable in today's global economy. In addition, as clients demand the expertise that comes with experience, firms can no longer afford to train their employees only to watch them leave.

Turnover and Retention Trends

According to a Catalyst, a New York-based non-profit group that studies workplace trends, factors that cause employees to leave their firms can be divided into two categories: "pull" and "push" factors. Pull factors arise from outside and include offers of high-paying jobs elsewhere, desire to pursue a life-long career dream, and family responsibilities. Push factors arise from within the current employer and can include a perceived disconnect between an employer's commitment to diversity and the execution of the practices that support that commitment, limited opportunities, lack of role models in senior leadership, unclear career paths, excessive workload due to bureaucratic and management inefficiencies, and lack of respect for personal life. Whereas employers have little control over pull factors, companies can help retain their workforce by focusing on the push factors over which they have significant control.

In a Catalyst study, senior-level women gave their top three reasons for which they would leave their current organization, with 42 percent citing increased compensation, 35 percent to accept the opportunity to develop new skills or competencies, and 33 percent to pursue greater advancement opportunities. High-level men gave the same reasons, with 51 percent citing increased compensation, 32 percent to accept the opportunity to develop new skills or competencies, and 30 percent to pursue greater advancement opportunities.

Although multiple studies and debates exist around the topic of measuring turnover, an accepted number for the cost of a professional or manager leaving a company is a minimum of one year's worth of salary and benefits, or at least 100% of the employee's salary and benefits. This formula measures the combined cost of termination, replacement, vacancy, and learning curve productivity loss.

Combating Turnover

The following chart shows that the rate of turnover from voluntary quits varies by industry, with the highest rate of quits in the leisure and hospitality industry and the lowest in the government.

Voluntary Quits by Industry, 2008

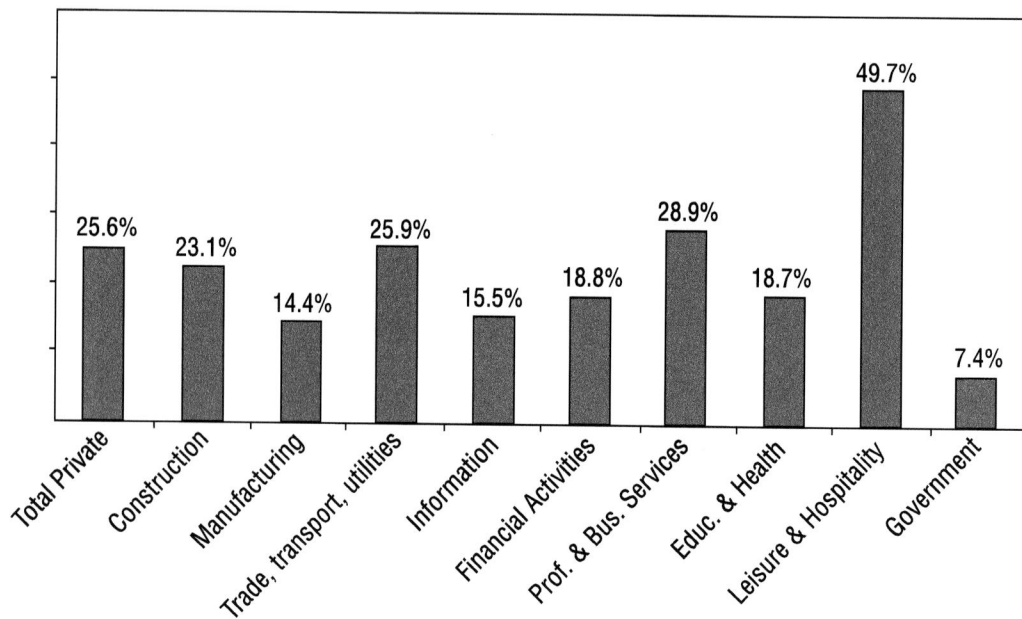

Source: Catalyst, 2008

To reduce turnover rates, Catalyst suggests companies first build awareness and more understanding regarding the experiences and perceptions of women and men of color by doing the following:

Assess the work environment.

- Find out about your organization's diversity strategy,
- Use internal surveys, focus groups, and interviews to document, by subgroup, the experiences, and perceptions of women and men of color.

Examine your own opinions, assumptions, and behavior.

- How inclusive are you about socializing with staff members from different backgrounds?

Examine what priority you give to institutional supports for staff members who are from backgrounds different from yours.

- Do your expectations for the performance of your staff that are of color vary from those for your other staff?

- Do you ever make assumptions based on stereotypes?

Develop closer relationships with women and men of color. Learn their perspectives.

- Make an effort to ask women and men of color about their perspectives, backgrounds, and interests

- Identify subgroups of women of color and men of color in your organization and go out of your way to learn about their unique experiences and challenges

- Increase understanding of differences and similarities between groups and within groups through education and informal dialogues, one-on-one and in groups

- Encourage differences in behavioral and work styles

Communicate and demonstrate your firm's commitment to diversity.

- Use training programs, one-on-one mentoring with senior leaders, inclusion in high-visibility programs, and networking opportunities

- Integrate diversity initiatives into routine organizational practices such as recruitment, orientation, training, career-development tools, and succession planning

- Hold managers accountable for the retention and advancement of women and men of color

- Create clearly articulated plans for long-term development of women and men of color

- Hold managers accountable for providing critical development opportunities and high-visibility assignments necessary for advancement

- Review managers' performance evaluations of subordinates by race/ethnicity and gender of subordinates

- Evaluate managers' performance and commitment. They communicate how managers will be evaluated over the course of the year for their input into succession planning

- Track overall effectiveness of diversity retention:
  * Women

  * Minorities

  * GLBT

  * Disabled

  * Ethnic groups

  * Immigrants

- Benchmark progress against goals and undertake gap analysis to solve problems

- Offer special programs from mentoring to day care and elder care

- Insure diverse candidate pool for upward mobility. Track succession planning results

- Use statistical analysis to set up succession planning initiatives and set up schedules

- Use surveys and results by demographics within the company or organization. They ask what employees expect; they solicit their feedback and aggregate the data

- Gain the support of managers and engage all areas of the workforce

- Use innovation and creativity as ways to increase diversity and with it, productivity

- Keep messages concise and programs focused

Effective Mentoring

Mentoring boosts retention and advancement, which explains why a Diversity Best Practices survey found that 80 percent of companies surveyed either had formal diversity mentoring programs or were in the process of establishing them. Mentoring not only helps employees' career tracks, but it is also an effective way to measure their internal impact.

Some elements of effective mentoring to consider when establishing a program include:

- Commit to mentoring programs and vision
- Develop principles, guidelines, and practices
- Confirm definitions as to types of formal and informal mentoring programs

- Mentor-Mentee Match Program: This system consists of one-on-one relationships that enhance personal and professional growth, improve cultural competency, assure skill building, and increase networking opportunities

- The Peer-Mentor Program: This may be a short-term program where a new employee is assigned to a current employee to familiarize the new employee to the organization

- Establish goals for each part of the program (i.e., high potentials, young professionals, self-selected, etc.)

- Seek champions and sponsors of the mentoring program

- Tie the program to organizational development

- Ensure staff accountability and infrastructure to support the program

- Confirm budget support for the mentoring program

- Build effective matchmaking

- Conduct training and education of mentors and mentees

- Provide orientation for mentor/mentee matches

- Add tools and resources

- Expose to senior management through structure activities

- Hold focus and discussion groups

- Assess communications, the intranet and a library of motivational and inspirational books and other educational materials

- Tie in communications support and implement with technology and other means

- Ensure tracking, monitoring and reporting

- Develop measurement and matrices for results

- Consider an innovative and significant approach as the program builds, including rewards and recognition

What type of mentoring is right for your organization? Do your employees' needs require formal or informal mentoring? The chart below offers some potential challenges and opportunities offered by each approach.

Informal Mentoring	Formal Mentoring
Low expectations make mentoring easier, but less effective	More challenging to do
Little or no training needed	Training required
Employees often don't ask for help for fear of appearing "dumb"	Employees feel questions are expected and so ask more questions and reveal needs
Experienced employees often don't help since they don't want to look like "know-it-alls"	Veterans know collaboration is desired and expected
Veterans don't want to intrude and don't want to appear critical or negative	Mentors are prepared to handle the challenges with finesse and skill
Individual informal help is hard to identify and hard to support, affirm and recognize	The organization knows who to support and to reward for helping
The need to be productive overwhelms desire to use time to learn and help others	Time for adult learning is more protected and more expected
Veterans support tends to further the status quo rather than new practices	Results improve as adult learning becomes better supported and more routine

The Procter & Gamble Company provides a strong corporate example of combining their employee resource group and mentoring efforts for maximum success. Procter & Gamble's Employee Association of Gay Men, Lesbians, Bisexuals, and Transgenders (EAGLES) has developed a mentoring program that provides support and guidance for individuals who are "coming out" in the workplace. This program specifically helps to foster support for any friend or family member who has self-identified as LGBT.

The Black Advertising Leadership Team (BALT) at Procter & Gamble also serves in an advocacy role through its mentoring initiatives. Through BALT, marketing directors and brand managers take the initiative to mentor and coach less senior members, helping them to navigate and succeed within the company. This professional interest overlaps with personal friendships creating sincere advocates.

Citigroup Inc. also is a leader in retaining and developing employees through mentoring. Thanks to ongoing participation of the senior leadership, Citi's mentoring program continues to inspire and help train employees. Citi offers several mentoring programs beyond traditional one-on-one mentoring. One example is "Coaching for Success," where participants are assigned both a coach and a "thinking partner"—an individual who helps guide the participant through issues and challenges. Participants are offered programs emphasizing self-awareness, career management, communication, and presentation skills. They also receive tips and feedback on styles of delivery, cross-cultural communication, the importance of building a network, and the value of diversified career moves.

Career Development and Succession Planning

A company's best resource is its people. The lifeline of an organization, strong employees are equipped with the talent that enables a company to pursue and secure new business growth, expand existing services, and devise innovative techniques and tools that enhance quality of life. Without pioneering, skilled, and dedicated talent, an organization becomes stagnant and stale. Having the right people on board—especially those who perform at high levels and exhibit true dedication and career investment in their corporations—will propel progress and growth.

As most companies know, recruiting and retaining top talent is a time consuming yet highly critical process that directly affects the ultimate success of an organization. Not only is the goal to obtain employees that are an ideal fit for the institution as a whole, but also for their particular positions and teams. The objective of career development is to retain diverse talent and support career development of employees worldwide, thus increasing the profitability and success of the organization.

Moreover, with the look and feel of the workforce changing, diverse employees are altering the cultural landscape of how Americans do business at home and abroad. Businesses that are adept at tapping great talent will have in their corner motivated individuals who rethink, reshape, decipher, and disseminate intelligent new strategies that speak directly to the values and cultures of our multifaceted consumer base.

Senior managers and executives who clearly understand that career development and succession planning are a management imperative systematically identify high-potential internal talent. These leaders proactively begin the process of nurturing that talent for larger responsibilities within the organization. Ultimately, career development and succession planning help to ensure that replacements are available to assume critically important positions as they become vacant.

In a survey conducted by AARP, 400 New York-based businesses were studied to determine how they deal with the departure and/or retention of older workers. The results revealed the importance of retaining instructional knowledge that might be lost when employees retire or otherwise leave. However, only a third of the businesses from the study reported having a formal process that enables employees who retire or leave to share the knowledge they have obtained on the job. The Bureau of Labor Statistics further states that by 2010, more than half of the workers in the United States will be over age 40.

In addition to aiding in the quick and effective filling of vacant positions by highly qualified talent, career development and succession planning initiatives both provide an opportune time for a corporation to review and analyze its diversity structure. Across the board, exceptional females and minorities continue to struggle with advancement in corporate

America, and women of color face the tallest barriers despite the fact that they are an increasing force in top workplaces across the nation.

Through reflection and foresight, companies that want to maintain a competitive advantage in today's global marketplace must ask: Are we providing opportunities for growth and development within our diverse network of employees, particularly for women and minorities, who continue to face various degrees of challenges and barriers in the corporate workplace? What safeguards do we have in place to support, train, and retain these assets?

The following 10-point plan offers suggestions for actively retaining and advancing female and minority employees through thoughtful career development and succession planning processes:

- **Make a commitment.** Commit to diversity succession planning to increase minorities in the management and divisional leadership in business units.

- **Set clear objectives.** Set objectives overall and then spread responsibility for the succession program so that all are aware of and understand the program.

- **Learn from others.** Study what others are doing; benchmark results against others in your industry.

- **Utilize measurement and evaluation tools.** Set up benchmarking, evaluation and measurement processes to analyze succession planning programs.

- **Outline competencies.** Understand and communicate required competencies needed to advance.

- **Define and communicate goals.** Clearly define how you can better the corporate culture.

- **Create a scorecard.** Profile current retention levels and develop a scorecard (trends and projections)—senior level, upward mobility, attrition reality and potential, climate survey results.

- **Determine the minority talent pool for management spots.** (i.e., current internal pool; where external recruitment may be essential to fill the numbers).

- **Leverage existing programs and knowledge.** Determine how to leverage current programs; determine retention rates for Hispanics, African Americans, Asian Americans, others.

- **Discuss customized 360-degree evaluation tools.** Create candidate profiles; compare overall scores on these profiles for minority and majority candidates.

Retaining and Developing Women of Color

In the race for top corporate talent across all levels, women of color are an imperative, yet vastly underutilized, business resource. Hiring and retaining women of color is not simply an issue for women of color. With increasing globalization, it makes good business sense to develop strategies to ensure that women of color thrive. Their leadership can be the key to exploring new markets, increasing consumer loyalty, adding creativity and diversity in decision making, and providing fresh insights into a growing consumer base.

The challenge facing corporations today is to make an honest and critical assessment of internal policies and procedures that either help or hinder the fair and valuable succession of women of color. While internal reflection and critique is often avoided, corporations who are not on the cutting edge of succession planning and who do not take the necessary steps to ensure an equitable and business savvy process will be on the losing end of progress.

An effective succession plan for women of color takes into account their goals and aspirations for personal and professional growth in conjunction with the company's goals and aspirations for business growth. It has to be a mutually beneficial partnership. Mechanisms should be in place to provide talented women with access to internal resources (e.g. mentors, sponsors, training) that can benefit their rise within the organization. Visibility is also essential, which means they should be exposed to assignments that provide the best possible display of their talents and abilities as potential leaders.

What is ideal is that these women have the ability to guide the global outreach for their companies and navigate into areas that offer promise, growth, and revenue building. For example, the spending power of the multicultural community is vast, and companies that are positioned to capitalize on the billions being dispensed can position their company for growth within these marketing niches. The Selig Center for Economic Growth at the University of Georgia's Terry College of Business recently released information on the growing spending trends among Blacks, Hispanics, Asians and Native Americans.

- African-American spending power was $845 billion in 2007 and is expected to rise to $1.1 trillion in 2012.

- Hispanic spending power has risen from $212 billion in 1999 to $869 billion in 2007 and is expected to be almost 1.1 trillion in 2012.

- Asian buying power has the second fastest projected rate of growth behind Hispanic buying power. Asian spending power was $253 billion in 2001, $459 billion in 2007, and is expected to grow to $670 billion by 2012.

- Native American buying power was $57 billion in 2007 and is expected to rise to $77 billion in 2012.

From an economic standpoint, companies that have women of color in decision making roles can bring clarity, creativity, vision, and diversity of thought and perspective. Having employees that can impact and influence these marketing segments can be a valuable asset to any company. As it stands, there is less than a handful of women of color currently heading Fortune 500 companies.

Corporations seeking a deep foothold in new and emerging markets can learn a thing or two by observing these leading women, and in turn, should take a strong look at their own women of color as they move to promote internally. Andrea Jung, for example, has propelled Avon's sales to almost $10 billion in 2007, from $4 billion when she first assumed the top post in 1999. She was also recently named to Apple's exclusive eight-member Board of Directors.

Today, Avon has nearly 5 million women sales employees in over 100 countries, including in emerging markets like China, India and Russia. With Jung as its lead trailblazer, Avon has experienced tremendous growth in China, a market which previously did not have an open-door policy for selling cosmetics door-to-door. There is no doubt that having a Mandarin-speaking CEO familiar with the global possibilities for new markets & new business growth assisted Avon in opening portals for consumer selling—both in China and worldwide.

Given the tremendous success of women of color in global business, one would expect to see more women moving up the corporate ranks in organizations big and small. Yet, major progress has yet to be seen. All employees want to feel valued, useful and productive, and women of color are no different; however, they are often challenged by exclusionary tactics that hinder their ability to be effective managers.

Corporate environment is a key area that continues to challenge the ability of women of color to function at full capacity. A company's environment encompasses many things, including the climate of inclusion, sense of support and investment in employees, opportunities for personal and professional development, respect for culture and family, and communicated dedication to work/life balance. Many corporations may talk of a strong commitment to diversity and inclusion, but too often their actions fail to support these aspirations in the workforce and C-suite.

Barriers to Advancement for Women of Color

Women of color tend to experience barriers when they are challenged from within their corporation through:

- **An inability to identify an influential sponsor, or mentor, within the organization.**
  Nearly all people in executive ranks have had someone help them along the way, someone who can speak on their behalf at meetings or guide them through the corporate maze of managerial development. If a woman of color is not in the pipeline to be recognized, she won't be. The presence of senior role models and mentors is a significant factor in the ability of organizations to retain top talented women of color.

- **The absence of informal networking opportunities with influential colleagues.** Networking is critical to advancement. In order for women of color to effectively showcase their professional skills and talents, they must first be recognized. High-level networking provides the opportunity for these women to make key connections that can rapidly and positively affect their professional development journey.

- **Lack of company role models who are members of their racial and ethnic group.** Being able to look "up" and see other faces such as ones' own is important for any employee seeking to advance within a company. If a woman of color can identify a role model who is not only a corporate leader, but who also reflects her image, advancement appears more tangible. This can lead to confidence and a greater likelihood of reaching out for support.

- **Omission from high-visibility assignments.** High-profile projects and responsibilities are the ones that get noticed. If a woman of color is not receiving assignments that allow her to effectively demonstrate her range and ability as a potential leader, how can she expect to get noticed or considered for promotion? Trust factors often come into play as women of color are often questioned in their ability to handle important projects or interact well with clients or colleagues outside of their own culture.

- **Balancing work and family.** Women typically shoulder a disproportionate share of the burden of balancing work and family, and often their careers can suffer as a result. Women of color working in corporate America who request work/life options from their supervisors can be judged unfairly. This is especially true when their supervisors may not understand the cultural context of their personal and family dynamics. Instead of being given the benefit of the doubt, women of color can be mislabeled as lazy, pushy, or ungrateful workers with attitude.

These challenges only represent some of the issues women of color contend with on a daily basis, and these challenges can create tensions that are only resolved by their departure from the company. When highly qualified women of color leave their organizations, the bottom-line impact on the company is costly and unnecessary. These women are heading to the exits because they cannot envision a future in a corporation that espouses diversity and inclusion in talk, yet excludes them from opportunities that could further their careers as well as benefit the company.

"Corporations may never fully diversify until they find ways to retain the minority workers in their ranks," observes Peter Hom in his paper, "Challenging Conventional Wisdom about Who Quits: Revelations from Corporate America." Minority women quit jobs more often than both whites and men of their own ethnicity, states Hom, and more specifically, African American women quit at a rate 61.2 percent greater than white men, and Hispanic women quit at a rate 67.5 percent greater than white men.

By providing the right support, opportunities and respect to these women, companies can ultimately retain top talent with the experience, drive, and perspective to be outstanding and long-term corporate leaders.

To implement a strategic plan, organizations need the right people in the right places at the right times. Without the intellectual and human capital, strategic plans cannot be realized. Therefore, succession planning and leadership identification is critical to the successful implementation of the organization's strategy. There is not a singular, universal approach that works well across all companies. Rather, effective companies match their succession strategies to their business goals.

Ultimately, succession planning should reflect the way an organization needs to change in order to achieve its strategic goals. When done well, it impacts the success of the company, at headquarters and in each of the operating companies or levels. The following is a list of key strategies corporations can use to ensure an effective succession plan:

- **Broaden your horizons.** If succession planning is to be real, people have to accept that those who are different can be effective leaders. Diversity departments should work with executives and managers to change current recruitment and promotion systems. Companies have to accept that women and minorities can succeed and make contributions to the leadership of the company or organization, even if they do not look like or manage like the current group.

- **Commit from the top**. Top management participation and support makes for a successful succession planning program. CEO and C-suite involvement motivates participants and ensures other members of the top management team devote time and effort to the succession planning program. When the CEO commits to diversity in succession planning, it will receive more attention and buy-in throughout the company.

- **Dedicate roles and responsibility.** Best practices companies hold someone or a team responsible for achieving the goals of the succession planning program. Many corporate directors and board members become actively involved. Roles and responsibilities should be clearly delineated.

- **Establish criteria for advancement.** Define and communicate clearly the criteria, process and expectations for upward mobility. Review them with the candidates. Taking the time to think through and communicate clear expectations is vital to ensuring the most qualified candidates from a diverse pool are included in succession planning.

- **Communicate internally.** The succession plan must become a part of the company's culture. Workshops should be held for managers across all levels of the company to understand why the company is undertaking this process, how it will work and what the desired outcome will be.

- **Facilitate mentoring and sponsorship relationships.** The mentoring relationship is a vital one to succession planning. It requires a sound and caring advisor – an astute individual who can assist in the process and who can expertly navigate the system. A sponsor can ensure that an employee's career plan is reviewed on a consistent basis.

- **Support and encourage self-nomination.** Best practices companies drive individual employees toward reaching goals and achieving positive results through developmental activities. Best practices companies that consider self-nomination procedures and systems encourage women and people of color to advance themselves and their interests.

- **Extend succession planning to all levels.** The most successful succession planning programs do not restrict succession planning to its top brass, but instead extend it to all levels. The greatest emphasis is placed at the lowest management levels where most positions and people exist or on the levels where the business need is the greatest.

- **Establish familiarity to retain institutional knowledge.** Large companies use succession development programs to familiarize future leaders with the corporate environment. Identifying and training existing junior talent, and guiding them with the help of current company leaders, will allow a smooth transfer of knowledge and ensure future success.

- **Learn from others while also assessing yourself.** Study what others are doing while also setting up benchmarking, evaluation and measurement processes to analyze succession planning programs. Benchmarking in best practices companies is tailored to the unique culture of the individual company. In many companies the CEO is personally involved and often holds him or herself responsible for the success of the program.

Survey Results: What Women of Color Want

For the past seven years, *Working Mother* has celebrated companies with cutting-edge policies and practices that support African-American, Asian-American, Latina and Native American women. The Working Mother Best Companies for Multicultural Women's initiative highlights the most important issues in the workplace for multicultural women, from understanding how identity impacts one's career to creating strategic alliances at work. Through the Working Mother Multicultural Women's National Conference and Regional Town Halls, *Working Mother* tracks what multicultural women would set as the top priority for their company. The answer? Accountability. More than one third of respondents said companies need to hold managers accountable for advancing multicultural women. Offering mentor programs and critical assignments were tied for second place, with 22 percent of the votes. Other findings include:

- **Networking styles:** When we asked multicultural women about their primary workplace networks, all racial/ethnic groups, except African American women, listed Caucasian women as their primary network. However, for 38% of African-American women, their primarily network was with women of their own race. Latinas and Multiracial women reported that they network primarily with men.

- **Mentors and sponsors:** The No. 1 most serious problem related to race/ethnicity and gender in the workplace, reported by 38% of attendees, was a lack of formal mentors and sponsors. Our winning companies recognize this, and 100% of the 2007 Working Mother Best Companies for Multicultural Women offer formal mentoring programs to their women of color employees.

- **Trust: Perhaps the most surprising data was on trust.** While women of color tended to trust their own race first and other women of color second, all groups concurred that they did not trust Caucasian women—even though white women were the most-named race/gender for role models, by 40% of respondents. This came as a surprise to many Caucasian women attendees—and provided an opportunity for learning.

- **Authenticity: When asked whether they had separate identities at home and on the job because of their race/ethnicity, 63% of Caucasian women reported that they did not.** By contrast, the largest groups, by percentage, believing they needed two personas were Native American and Multiracial women. Half of African American women said they maintain separate identities. About one-third of the Asian-American women and Latinas also reported feeling the pressure to maintain separate lives.

Succession Planning and Women of Color

Succession planning is a critical aspect of any business that looks to lead in the twenty-first century. Women of color are making gains, with more than five million women of color now holding managerial and professional positions in the workforce. Yet, they account for only 1.7 percent of corporate officers and top earners in the Fortune 500 companies.

Women of color should be able to enter the workforce expecting an equitable corporate culture. Having earned relevant degrees and gained valuable experiences, it is not unreasonable for women of color to expect access to opportunities that will support and advance their career goals. The factors that affect their retention, development and advancement are predicated on the company's commitment to diversity initiatives and an inclusive work environment.

Corporations invested in succession planning programs that identify and groom high-potential women of color to run operations will move to the head of the pack as our workplaces and marketplaces continue to rapidly diversify. Evaluating the succession planning process with a focus on supporting a more diverse talent pool is critical. And best-practice companies that earn high grades with women of color do so because they collectively embody the idea of creating a business environment that motivates women of color to aim higher in their business goals while providing the resources and genuine support to assist them in this effort.

True succession planning covers the gamut of recruitment, retention, and advancement. To create a successful program, remember to be inclusive from the get go, and recruit from a variety of sources. Make a strong commitment to diversity and inclusion, and instill this commitment throughout corporate culture. Provide ongoing career development for all groups, not just women of color, and offer powerful networking and mentoring opportunities that are not just lateral, but that allow for access to top leaders as well. Measure your results and hold executives across the board accountable. And finally, see and treat women and minorities as the true corporate assets they are, and spread this knowledge and action by leading as an example for others.

Conclusion

In this chapter, we:

• Discussed the representation of minorities and women in the United States.

• Evaluated how best practices companies recruit and retain minorities and women.

• Examined key ways to retain and develop women of color.

• Reviewed why employees, particularly minorities and women, leave or stay.

• Assessed the impact mentoring has on recruitment, retention, and advancement.

• Explored current trends in career development and succession planning.

Through our examination of diversity and inclusion through the lenses of representation, recruitment, retention, and development, we can conclude that the representation of minorities and women in the country is increasing overall. What remains starkly evident, however, is that parity has yet to be achieved, particularly in the upper ranks of the workforce where the dominant demographic is still white and male.

Yet parity encompasses much more than mere representation. Many companies focus on diversity recruitment—or, getting minority and female candidates "in the door"—but best-practice companies set themselves apart by viewing recruitment as only the first step of many. These trailblazing organizations inherently believe that having a diverse workforce—in terms of gender, ethnicity, ability, faith, age, and other characteristics—leads to greater innovation, energy, teamwork, and ultimately, business growth.

The real question, then, shifts from how to attract minority and female candidates to how to keep them on board and nurture their growth within the organization. Retention and development initiatives can take numerous forms, including those discussed in this chapter and in the subsequent case studies, such as formalized mentoring, diversity training, employee networks and resource groups, structured succession planning processes, and work/ life programs. The key is to analyze current strengths and gaps, determine the programs and initiatives that can address weak areas, and commit—through financial resources, time, dedicated roles, leadership buy-in, and measurement.

Case Study: Medtronic, Inc.

Medtronic, Inc. sets the standard in global medical technology, doing business in 120 countries with more than 37,000 employees and headquarters in the United States, Japan, and Switzerland. Its well-known mission is "to alleviate pain, restore health, and extend life." But Medtronic is quickly gaining worldwide recognition for a different commitment—its commitment to being a globally and culturally diverse workplace. Diversity is seen an important international business strategy. The company offers resources, support groups, mentor programs, and seminars to foster an inclusive atmosphere among employees.

The results are clear. There are nearly 12,000 employees outside of the U.S. Additionally, women comprise 46 percent of the workforce, and minorities represent 24 percent.

Medtronic approaches employee diversity with mentoring as a means of recruitment. Awareness Benefiting Leadership and Employees with Disabilities (ABLED) is an employee diversity special interest group and mentor program. Medtronic hosts students for Disability Mentoring Day. It utilizes members of the Society of Hispanic Professional Engineers (SHPE), National Society of Black Engineers (NSBE), and Society of Women Engineers (SWE) to create internal organizations which then work with existing employee resource groups. Overall, these initiatives emphasize awareness of the professional organizations and are strong sources for recruiting when coupled with Medtronic's constant presence at minority career fairs.

The next stage is employee education, specifically the Diversity Learning Initiative "You Make the Difference," which teaches inclusion and respect along with productivity. It begins with a play, "Lazarus," that encourages pluralism and equality while exploring prejudices based on race, ethnicity, class, and profession. It continues with eight hours of classroom training about awareness and acceptance. More than 98 percent of all Medtronic employees have been through the program. They emerge from the initiative with more cultural awareness and the ability to effectively interact with all employees, customers, suppliers, and stakeholders.

Medtronic understands that education is not enough and cares for its employees the same way the employees care for consumers. Medtronic offers domestic partner health benefits and often hosts wellness programs about women's health issues and parenting. It provides training on cultural sensitivity, English as a second language, and conversational English. When collecting employee feedback and suggestions on initiatives and diversity, it utilizes seven languages.

Employees feel safe and appreciated in the diverse work environment. "I have a passion for the people that work in my area. They are a diverse group, and it is wonderful to share their cultures and ideas, and to find out that, truly, we are all very similar," said an assembly worker.

Medtronic also supports diversity outside of the company by sponsoring groups like National Organization of Gay and Lesbian Scientists and Technical Professionals (NOGLSTP), a non-profit organization that works to eliminate discrimination against LGBT scientists, engineers, and technical professionals. The Medtronic Foundation allocates 20 percent of all contributions for education, specifically focusing on programs that encourage minorities and women to participate in underrepresented fields. Both of these tasks promote diversity in Medtronic's field which translates to a higher talent pool of minority workers.

Case Study: Novartis

To operate successfully as a global organization, it is essential that Novartis' people reflect the rich cultural, ethnic and gender diversity of its markets. As the company's customer base becomes increasingly diverse, a diverse talent pool becomes a critical bridge between the workplace and the marketplace. Diversity of its workforce enhances customer insight and our ability to meet the needs of patients and other stakeholders.

Novartis considers diversity and inclusion to encompass, but not be limited to:

- Ethnicity

- Gender

- Thinking styles

- Religion and belief

- Sexual orientation

- Age

- Physical ability

- Education

- Nationality

- Life experiences

By many measures, Novartis already is a highly diverse organization. The Corporate Executive Group (CEG) includes 27 nationalities. The proportion of female CEG members employed by Novartis Group companies worldwide has climbed to nearly 20% from 10% in 2005. Two of the 11 members of the Novartis Board of Directors are women. There has been notable improvement at Sandoz, Novartis' generic pharmaceuticals Division, where women now comprise almost 21% of CEG members employed by Group companies in the Sandoz Division, up from zero only three years ago. The Novartis Institutes for BioMedical Research, the company's pharmaceutical research unit, also have seen a rapid transformation, with women now comprising 18% of the CEG population employed by Group companies of NIBR, compared to 8% in 2005.

Diversity and Inclusion Advisory Council

The Diversity and Inclusion Advisory Council (DIAC), created in 2006, comprises a group of external experts who advise Novartis on development and implementation of diversity and inclusion strategies and practices. In addition to academics, the DIAC includes businesspeople with direct experience of establishing diversity programs in global businesses. DIAC members also hold open meetings with associates and meet semiannually with Novartis business and diversity leaders to both support and objectively challenge company activities and progress.

Talent Review

Divisions and business units have developed strategies and action plans for diversity and inclusion, based on local situations and business cases. Targets for diversity and inclusion have been integrated into objectives of senior Novartis managers around the world.

"The next generation of Novartis leaders will be more diverse and global," says Juergen Brokatzky-Geiger, Ph.D., Head of Human Resources and member of the Executive Committee of Novartis. To attract and retain scarce talent, employee engagement will be a top priority. International surveys indicate that corporate citizenship programs as well as diversity and inclusion strategies are key drivers of employee engagement, along with opportunities to improve skills and capabilities, areas in which Novartis scores above benchmarks and norms.

The well-established global Organization and Talent Review (OTR) process enables Novartis to identify, assess, and develop associates with high potential. In 2008, 76% of the open positions at the Corporate Executive Group (CEG) level—the 350 most senior executives at Novartis—were filled with internal candidates, underscoring the company's focus on internal development of talent.

Diversity and inclusion initiatives aim to make Novartis better reflect the heterogeneity of customers and stakeholders around the world. "A diverse organization is more likely to be a creative environment because the ability to learn new things often comes from differences in views, backgrounds and beliefs," says Daniel Vasella, M.D., former chairman and chief executive officer of Novartis. "We have to do an even better job of bringing in people from geographies where we have a large and growing presence but under representation in management and leadership. We have a responsibility to ensure not only that they are identified, but also supported, so they can grow within the organization."

Global Diversity: Brazil

At the beginning of the decade, Brazil adopted legislation requiring companies to step up recruitment of people with disabilities. At all companies in Brazil with more than 1,000 employees, individuals with disabilities should comprise a minimum of 5% of the workforce. Failure to comply with the new law can result in penalties, including heavy fines and exclusion from government tenders for healthcare products.

The Novartis organization in Brazil had only two disabled employees prior to passage of the law, but an aggressive recruitment campaign added more than 80 individuals with disabilities to the payroll, close to the 5% target that must be reached by December 2009. The majority has physical disabilities, including impaired hearing and vision, but the Brazilian unit also has hired two employees with learning disabilities.

The new recruits have been deployed across the Novartis organization in Brazil in many customer-facing positions as well as in production and back-office jobs. More than 20% of the disabled employees are sales representatives, and many have forged unusually close relationships with the healthcare professionals on whom they call.

Successfully integrating people with disabilities into teams across the company "has expanded the experience of associates, and enriched the spirit and culture of Novartis in Brazil," says Alexander Triebnigg, Head of both the Country Organization and Country Pharmaceuticals Organization in Brazil. "And it sends a positive signal about diversity and inclusion to the public, government agencies and customers."

Chapter 9

Training and Education

Contributor: Eric Manson
Vice President, Diversity & Inclusion, inVentiv Health

Just as diversity-specific training cannot thrive in a vacuum absent of a comprehensive diversity and inclusion strategy, diversity and inclusion training too will fail to be effective if it is not an integral part of a broader corporate training process. In establishing a D&I training strategy, a company should first examine how corporate learning happens today. Secondly, it should consider different types of deliver vehicles and how they impact corporate performance objective learning.

Whatever the method used in diversity and inclusion training, the primary goal is to create an ongoing awareness and understanding of human diversity as a corporate asset. However, awareness and understanding is not enough. For diversity and inclusion training to be truly effective, it must also teach employees how to leverage their own diversity and the diversity of others to support the success of the company through inclusion.

In this chapter, we will explore the following questions:

• What are the current challenges and obstacles to diversity and inclusion training?

• How has globalization impacted diversity and inclusion training?

• What are the various types of diversity and inclusion training?

• What are the characteristics of effective diversity and inclusion training programs?

• What content should be included in diversity and inclusion training?

Challenges, Barriers, and Trends

Many of the challenges facing diversity training programs are not unique to diversity. It is important to be aware of them as not to misdiagnose them as diversity-specific issues. Indeed, it is interesting to see that training in general faces the challenge of business alignment, much like Diversity & Inclusion initiatives in general.

The most prevalent obstacle to diversity training is time, and when coupled with organizational right-sizing, workloads, etc., this can become even more pronounced. Lack of time may not necessarily be main culprit, but rather a lack of demonstrating the importance of diversity training and how it ties to business objectives. When individuals are not ready for change they often view the associated costs of time and effort as greater than the benefits. Thus, linking diversity training to the organization's business goals and the corporate D&I strategy are important to diffuse this issue. The following list shows the top challenges facing today's organizations taken from 786 companies. According to researchers, six reasons organizations resist D&I training:

1. Employees are unclear about the changes and what to expect.

2. Different people see different meanings in the proposed changes.

3. Managers and supervisors are torn between the pressures of making change and strong opposing forces preferring things remain they way they have always been.

4. Employees who feel pressured to change resist more so than if they are involved somehow in the planning process.

5. Resistance rises when changes are made based on personal reasons as oppose to impersonal ones.

6. The organizational culture is not taken into consideration.

Additionally, the following miscues can happen during training that will create barriers:

- Trainers are not competent and fluent at facilitating and presenting

- Trainers use their own psychological issues, like trust or group affiliation, as templates for training

- Trainers have political agendas

- Training is not integrated into the organization's overall approach to D&I

- Training is too brief, too late, or too reactive to a bad situation like legal action

- Training does not distinguish among the different meanings of valuing D&I, pluralism, EEO, Affirmative Action, and communicating across cultures

- Training uses a limited definition of whose differences should be valued

- Training is based on a philosophy of political correctness or moral obligation

- Training forces people to reveal their feelings about their colleagues or participate in activities that do not respect one's dignity or differences

- Individual styles or participation is not respected

- Only one group is pressured to change

- Resource material is used referencing outdated views

- Trainers do not model the skills or philosophy parallel with valuing D&I

- Content covers an insufficient number of issues and does not engage people on an individual basis

- The curriculum is not tailored to attendees' needs or is not matched to the skills and experience of the trainer

- Trainers are chosen because they represent or are advocates for a minority group

- Training does not make the link between stereotyping behavior and personal or organizational effectiveness

- Trainers are insensitive, have no credibility, and do not engender trust

- Training is presented as remedial and the attendees as individuals with problems

- Training is too shallow or too deep

- The discussion of the tough issues like transgenderism, spirituality, and reverse discrimination are prohibited

- Trainers are usually women or ethnic minorities

- Emphasis is on sensitizing white males

- Awareness is the sole objective

- Programs are guilt-driven

- Trainers focus on the how of communication versus what is said or intended

- Orientation is toward the past and the future while ignoring the present where the change of action must transpire

In order to compete and gain a competitive advantage, today's organizations must remain on the cutting edge of innovation, products, services, and training. We must find a way to update our inventory of skills and competencies so that we become as fluent in the new order of things as we have been in the past.

Globalization and Diversity Training

Today, globalization touches all areas of an organization's operation and structure, including D&I. Global diversity is causing our society to move from a homogenous to a heterogeneous one. This can lead to a combination of challenges like confusion, increased complexity, ambiguity, ethnocentrism, stereotyping, and cultural bias. Organizations now need not just a new set of interpersonal and communication skills but fluency in them to succeed in this global climate. Many agree that a key component of diversity is not only our similarities and differences but equally the anxieties and tensions that naturally accompany them. Diversity practitioners' challenge is to provide a framework through training for organizations to positively and proactively manage these anxieties while leading to productive business outcomes.

Best Practices and Strategies

Types of Diversity Training

Diversity training generally falls into three categories: awareness-based, skills-based, and integration-based. Evidence supports a combined approach, but one must employ these schemes based on the intimate knowledge, understanding, and uniqueness of one's organization to maximize their effectiveness and business impact.

Awareness-based training programs are the most popular of the three approaches. The primary objectives are to provide information about diversity in general, heighten awareness and sensitivity through uncovering hidden assumptions and biases, assess attitudes and values, correct myths and stereotypes, and foster individual and group sharing. Additionally, some programs focus on providing demographic data and demonstrating the benefits to the workforce. They may also touch on barriers that employees encounter and use the training to demonstrate the organization's commitment to diversity. And lastly, and perhaps most relevant today, is making and reinforcing the business case for D&I.

Awareness is the beginning of framing a common understanding and some expectations so when organizations discuss D&I everyone has a common reference point. This does not mean there is universal acceptance and agreement, but that the context in which these issues are discussed or applied is moving forward. This aspect of diversity training is critical to the bigger picture, but one should understand that it alone is not the answer and in some cases may cause more problems than it resolves if done in isolation. Employees need a toolbox of skills to implement in order to increase their productivity and effectiveness.

Skills-based training moves to action from awareness. It should provide individuals with an actionable framework in which to address the day-to-day challenges in a proactive and effective way so as to drive the organization's business forward. While these challenges and issues may have a diversity overtone to them, they are not black and white but rather varying shades of gray. Therefore, this cannot be a rigid checklist of steps to take or it becomes like putting a round peg into a square hole, and does not lead to the successful outcomes required in today's ever-changing business environment. Individuals must understand the context, content, and use of these learned skills. There are three key factors to consider in skills-based training, including: building new diversity-interaction skills, reinforcing existing skills, and inventory skill-building methodologies.

The third approach is integration-based training. While this is a separate approach, it touches on the awareness- and skills-based approaches previously discussed. There are many benefits to this approach, especially if one of the goals is integrating your Diversity & Inclusion strategy into the organization's existing training framework. This requires one to work in a close, collaborative way with the existing training department or team. This collaboration may help dampen some of the resistance individuals have based on their personal biases or prior experiences.

Given the challenges of time away from work and being overwhelmed with too many programs or initiatives at once, among other perceived drawbacks, integration-based training can increase the frequency with which D&I learning occurs. Furthermore, it allows one to see the broader application and how it relates to other relevant areas and complimentary programs within the organization. Again, it contributes to providing a process or framework so employees may consciously draw upon and apply these skills in the day-to-day context of doing business. This can help one to see where the diversity implications are both overt and implied.

Characteristics of Effective Diversity Training Programs

While one size does not fit all, there is some empirical evidence of what works. Following are 15 recommendations for creating an effective diversity training initiative from The Conference Board, a New York-based non-profit organization that studies management trends.

- **Create a supportive infrastructure.** Executive support is critical.

- **Provide clear communication about the training and how it relates to the over arching D&I corporate strategy.**

- **Create inclusive programs and processes.** It must be clear that D&I is about everyone and involves everyone. This should ideally have been addressed in your D&I vision, mission, and already established definitions of Diversity, etc.

- **Create flexibility and tailor to internal needs.** This is especially critical if your organization is spread over multiple geographies and has several independent business operating units.

- **Conduct train-the-trainer sessions.** This builds internal change agents that can continually support and help legitimize the initiative on a sustained basis. It will also provide additional avenues for maximizing impact and effectiveness.

- **Include senior management in training and require attendance.** They too help legitimize the importance of training and demonstrate that it is not merely the latest passing fad.

- **Enroll all employees.** This way, it is transparent to all and there is consistency in the messages conveyed. If, pending on how your organization has defined diversity, it involves everyone, then why wouldn't everyone be trained? You cannot hold people accountable for things which they do not know.

- **Train business units together.** All work is a collaborative team effort directly or indirectly. This team approach should be emphasized in training as well.

- **Provide trust and confidentiality.** Remember, you are taking people where they may not have been, and the unknown creates a certain amount of trepidation. That fear must be proactively managed up front or participants will not get the maximum, if any, benefits from the training.

- **Set clear training session ground rules.**

- **Co-facilitate sessions.** Take advantage of gender, ethnicity and having someone from the training team or HR.

- **Ensure diverse attendance.** If the departments split their attendance into groups ensure that each group has a representative mix of race, gender, age, and experience, etc.

- **Establish action plans.** This is the ultimate reason for implementing the skills-based approach. Inform participants upfront that they will be asked to 'act' on what they learn during the training. At the end of the session, spend some time brainstorming "action" steps while referencing specifics from the session.

- **Provide follow-up.** Not much is internalized after one occurrence. Constant and routine reminders, along with application, will lead to developing and sustaining the new behaviors.

- **Create accountability.** Consider having the attendees pair up for follow-up dialogue or to discuss fulfillment of the action plans.

Components of Effective Diversity Training Programs

- **Training for the sake of training provides no real benefits.** Training has a fundamental importance as one of the many facets of a comprehensive diversity strategy. Almost every functional aspect of a diversity initiative requires some type of training, education, or preparation on the part of the organization in order to help drive the organization's business objectives.

- **Training programs should be tailored to meet unique and individual needs of the organization.** Conduct a needs assessment before conducting training. This ensures critical areas of concern are addressed appropriately. Additionally, the training should compliment the organizational culture and climate.

- **Integrate with other initiatives.** There may be complimentary programs currently established where aspects of diversity training have a natural fit. This is not to dilute or soft step diversity, but, rather, a way to enhance the overall impact and facilitate internalization.

Managers and supervisors increase their effectiveness by improved recruiting and reducing turnover costs through decreased absenteeism. Perhaps most importantly, they provide a work environment that more closely reflects the organization's values and beliefs around its employees. They respect and recognize individuals in proportion to their contribution and treat them as unique individuals rather than stereotyping them. Employees who are sufficiently motivated to work can focus on accomplishing the business objectives and goals. They become more productive and successful—and success breeds success.

In the end, the organization as a whole improves in terms of collective teamwork, improved customer service, and effective communication. Reductions in training and employee turnover costs are realized, which impacts the bottom line.

Creating Training Programs

The Conference Board recommends asking the following questions when considering what to include in a diversity training program:

- How does diversity link to the business case?

- Is it awareness based?

- Is it about race, gender, or age?

- What's the current employee knowledge base surrounding diversity?

- Who will be your audience?

Research shows that most organizations focus first on programs that will improve interpersonal skills, followed by multicultural literacy. Next, the focus is on technical skills, and, lastly, sessions that emphasize corporate acculturation.

The type of employees to be trained should be examined as well. As you move through the organizational structure, priorities and business focus change, and it is important to deliver the training in an effective and relevant way so each and every person can individually acquire what they need in order to maximize their performance and impact.

The number of employees to be trained is equally an important consideration, especially where dialogue and group interaction is involved. While all employees should be trained, it is of value to examine how the basic components of training may be emphasized when training managers. Knowledge is a intellectual component that helps managers focus on developing the business case.

Regurgitating factoids and figures requires no great skill. Given the potential volatility and emotional connection that employees bring to the session, the trainer must be very adept at navigating these issues if and when they occur. They must diffuse those issues and maintain a positive and safe learning environment. This is not to dismiss the various other skills and competencies of subject matter expertise that also contribute to successful learning outcomes.

Trainers can be internal employees, external consultants, or a combination of both. There are pros and cons to each. An assessment and working knowledge of your organization and its culture—including size of the workforce, timetable, complexity of issues, employee receptivity, and budget—will help in determining which approach suits your company.

Conclusion

In this chapter, we:

• Assessed the current challenges and obstacles to diversity and inclusion training,

• Investigated how globalization has impacted diversity and inclusion training,

• Reviewed various types of diversity and inclusion training,

• Outlined the characteristics of effective diversity and inclusion training programs.

• Determined what content should be included in diversity and inclusion training.

Diversity and inclusion training has had its naysayers over the years who assert that D&I training can actually do more harm than good. But as with anything, a poorly planned and executed program will typically produce poor results, while a quality program will typically produce quality results.

For diversity and inclusion training to be effective, the right factors have to be present. To the greatest extent possible, diversity and inclusion training should be presented to employees in a way that makes them want to participate as opposed to making them feel forced. A truly comprehensive training program should also offer a wide variety of topics throughout the year and be provided on an ongoing basis. And finally, all training programs should appeal to different learning styles. The ultimate thing to keep in mind is that corporate diversity and inclusion is a journey. This chapter presented a framework for each organization to initiate the diversity and inclusion training process with a strong foundation of understanding.

Case Study: Target Corporation

Diversity and inclusion may begin with hiring the right people, but endurance and support requires training and education. This creates a safe and productive environment in which people thrive, and clients recognize this and vendors appreciate it. As globalization and diversity continue to grow, it is imperative that employees and senior management receive accurate and thorough training and education to acquire and practice necessary diversity and inclusion skills. Target Corporation works hard to stay one step ahead of its competition, and it does this effectively by recognizing the importance of diversity and education. The diversity of its employees reflects the diversity of its communities. However, once employed, employees learn the best methods for utilizing and taking advantage of diversity.

Target is dedicated to creating and maintaining a high-performing team with a wide array of strengths, backgrounds, and lifestyles. It defines diversity as individuality: age, race, gender, sexual orientation, language, religion, family, and education. Forty-two percent of Target team members are ethnic minorities and 59 percent are women. These numbers are both much higher than the national average. Target brings out the full potential of every individual through training, which enhances awareness of diversity in the workplace and builds the environment necessary for promoting diversity.

Target offers a series of classes, from "Appreciating Differences" to "Communication Styles." Each one not only teaches team members how to value diversity, but also promotes understanding of one another. Target employees can also choose from other classes in public speaking, time management, and communication skills. Within each class area, the individual courses are tailored to use various personality preference instruments to address style differences. Team members at the supervisory level also have leadership development classes. New team members are required to participate in training and education about the Corporate Diversity Mission. Target also offers more than 50 training items in Spanish, with all basic training materials published in both English and Spanish. Furthermore, when new employees begin at Target, they are given an individualized, detailed training and development plan that is applicable for the first 90 days of the new position. This ensures that diversity training and inclusion education is an integral part of all employee development.

The benefits of diversity training are twofold. They can be seen in the corporate world, affecting the bottom like. Diversity training improves recruitment efforts, increases employee retention rates, and reduces employee turnover. It leads to higher performance and productivity, both from individuals and the team. And it directly benefits employees by helping them build the skills and knowledge to function effectively in a multicultural environment. Through a conscious effort to implement diversity training, Target is experiencing these positive effects. It is working to combat racism, sustain an inclusive attitude, and improve the overall Target image and reputation.

Chapter 10

Employee Network and Affinity Groups

In corporate America, a common mission, vision, and purpose in thought and action across all levels of an organization is of the utmost importance to bottom line success; however, so is the celebration, validation, and respect of each individual. Combining these two fundamental areas effectively requires diligence, understanding, and trust from all parties—and one way organizations are attempting to bridge the gap is through employee network and affinity groups.

Network and affinity groups began as small, informal, self-started employee groups for people with common interests and issues. Also referred to as employee or business resource groups, among other names, these impactful groups have now evolved into highly valued company mainstays. Today, network and affinity groups exist not only to benefit their own group members; but rather, they strategically work both inwardly and outwardly to edify group members as well as their companies as a whole.

Today there is a strong need to portray value throughout all workplace initiatives. Employee network groups are no exception. To gain access to corporate funding, benefits and positive impact on return on investment needs to be demonstrated. As network membership levels continue to grow and the need for funding increases, network leaders will seek ways to quantify value and return on investment.

In its ideal state, network groups should support the company's efforts to attract and retain the best talent, promote leadership and development at all ranks, build an internal support system for workers within the company, and encourage diversity and inclusion among employees at all levels.

In this chapter, we will explore the following questions:

• What are the benefits of employee network and affinity groups to the company? To the employee?

• How do employee network and affinity groups impact recruitment, retention, and leadership and product development?

• What are the basics of employee network and affinity group operations, to include mission and vision, charters, funding and resources, programs, and visibility?

• What is the typical infrastructure of employee network and affinity groups?

• How should organizations measure the impact of employee network and affinity groups on the bottom line? What are the challenges? What tools can be used?

Benefits

Employee networks are a key part of a company's D&I strategy. They are effective tools for championing programs and people, a corporation's greatest asset. Employee networks may be composed of African Americans; Asian Americas; Hispanics; older workers; workers with disabilities; gay, lesbian, bisexual and transgendered people; women; members of religious denominations; global networks; and others. Open to all employees, each network typically has a formal structure with leaders, periodic meetings, and objectives, and often serves as an external advisory group.

In today's corporate quest for diverse talent and multicultural partnerships, employee resource groups are more important than ever in order to create a workforce that mirrors the face of the consumers to accelerate business results. The corporate environment has evolved to not only support network and affinity groups but to promote them. These groups aid in the attraction and retention of new hires. They help send the signal to the world that the organization values inclusivity which leads to innovation.

Leading companies take an active interest in their network and affinity groups. These companies provide speakers and sponsorships, ask networks to assist with recruiting and retention, and even ask them to help build market share. Strong groups have a purpose and a plan. They often give advice and counsel to the company and to the senior diversity and inclusion officer. These groups prosper with adequate budgets and management advice.

Affinity groups contribute to business success through several means: recruitment and retention, product development, creating a positive and supportive work environment and helping to deliver the commitment to diversity and inclusion to name a few. For example, at 3M, affinity groups serve as advisors to the product development division, while AT&T's employee resource groups have helped the company in its recruitment and retention efforts, and some groups have also provided a strong community influence through the adopt-a-school, scholarship, and mentoring programs. Taking the business of ERGs more seriously, Honeywell has its business resource groups sign partnership statements viewing these groups as actual business partners. These groups at Honeywell also help the company to understand business norms within other cultures, such as Asia.

Corporate network groups have a mission to represent the company. They are not only expected to operate like a department at some companies, but are also provided with an annual budget and sometimes an executive sponsor in order to push forward diversity and inclusion strategies. These groups provide the benefits of recruiting, mentoring and business growth. Most are involved in professional member development activities, business partnerships and community relations to help garner company recognition and support. They lead other employees toward better cultural understanding.

Employee networks have several distinct benefits for the company, including:

- **Establish/Revamp the Corporate Diversity Vision** Network groups can provide valuable viewpoints on corporate D&I policies and initiatives. They are often better able to locate areas in need of improvement and may suggest areas in need of policy or attention.

- **Aid in the Recruitment of Minority Employees** Corporate network groups can aid the corporation throughout this area by suggesting focuses of process improvements in areas such as recruitment, development, and retention of the minority workforce.

- **Connect with an Extended or New Consumer Base** Employee resource groups often have the means and enthusiasm to assist the corporation with sales goals and brand awareness. Specialized network groups are often excellent forums for idea generation and serve as wonderful sounding boards for targeted campaigns.

Recruitment, Retention, and Leadership Development

Employee resource groups aid in recruitment by helping companies gain perspectives on techniques that appeal to target populations. Merrill Lynch, for example, has demonstrated this practice with the company's Native American Professional Network. This group reaches out to students through programs and recruiting events throughout the United States.

However, diversity and inclusion is not just about getting people in the door, but about moving people up the corporate ladder—both at headquarters and throughout operating divisions. Employee resource groups can help to increase the percentage of women and minorities throughout the corporation. Membership helps create an inclusive environment and foster retention.

Ford has utilized its employee groups to help retain top talent. Ford's Parenting Network, for instance, has provided input on work/life balance and contributed to the now adapted work/life policies, such as adoption assistance, lactation policies, and other support.

In terms of professional development, it is important for minorities to see their peers in similar positions. YMCA, for example, maintains not only affinity groups, but also leadership networks. These groups have a similar focus, but concentrate on opportunities for development as individuals or as a group. These groups participate in career development, personal development, networking, training opportunities, and mentoring. YMCA maintains five affinity groups including the Hispanic/Latino Leadership Network and Affinity Group, African American Leadership Network and Executive Forum, Asian American Leadership Network and Affinity Group, Gay, Lesbian, Bisexual, Transgendered Leadership Network and Affinity Group, and the Women's Leadership Network and Affinity Group.

Additionally, YMCA's African American Leadership Network and Executive Forum strives to increase leadership development of African Americans through career development, personal development, networking, training opportunities, and mentoring. This group helps the YMCA recruit and retain top talent, provide employee training, and create mentoring opportunities.

Product Development

Employee resource groups are vital for targeting the sectors they represent through marketing, employee support, and product testing. Executives can call on groups for feedback on marketing campaigns and product development. These groups can therefore contribute to business objectives. For example, PepsiCo developed guacamole-flavored Doritos and soft drinks aimed at black consumers through contributing affinity groups, adding 1 percent to the corporate bottom line.

Ford also added to its bottom line through its Interfaith Network, which reached out to different churches to encourage purchases with discounts from friends and families of the employees, known as the Friends and Neighbors Program. This group brought more than $260 million in sales through this program. Another Ford initiative that generated product testing came through the Professional Women's Network. The company asked this group to test the seat height in their cars for women.

Marketing campaigns can by surveyed by employee resource groups to gauge the level of effectiveness. The Realize campaign of Verizon Communications/Wireless, launched in 2005, featured real customers pursuing their entrepreneurial dreams with the help of Verizon's broadband services. This campaign was created with the assistance of an employee resource groups for black employees, called the Consortium of Information and Telecommunications Executives (CITE). The Realize campaign generated three times the original sales goals in one year and expanded target cities. Verizon's decision to include its employees in this campaign shows the direct result of product development by employee resource groups.

Operations

In their ideal state, network groups should support the company's efforts to attract and retain the best talent, promote leadership and development at all ranks, build an internal support system for workers within the company, and encourage diversity and inclusion among employees at all levels. Moreover, networks should support career development and mentoring for its members, help each individual build upon their own personal network for success, and act as a guiding force in helping the corporation achieve work/life effectiveness.

Best Practices for Employee Network Groups:

- **Commitment and Direction** Offer a strong message of commitment from CEO/ Executive Leadership Team that is clear, consistent and communicated throughout the organization; clear appreciation for affinity group business case; direct CEO and senior leader involvement.

- **Authorized Groups** Reflect key employee constituencies and extending beyond race, gender, and sexual orientation to ability, faith, professional interests, and lifestyles; in addition to market segments, some drive eligibility off of Title VII classes.

- **Role of Affinity Group** Act as a "voice" for identity group; actively attract, develop, and retain talent; develop new business opportunities; promote the Brand; community outreach.

- **Integration** Play an integral role in the Diversity strategy; have "formal" linkages across corporate entities and functions to leverage affinity group as resource; help build leadership pipeline; have active partnership with business units.

- **Business Connection** Actively engage in driving business goals: talent recruitment/ retention; employee engagement, personal/professional development; emerging marketing; and being the "face" of the company in the community.

- **Organization** Offer corporate affinity groups with chapters by identity groups, across geography (regional, global), in some isolated cases aligned with business segments; affinity groups well connected with each other and the organization.

- **Governance** Offer corporate standards with guidelines, bylaws and operating agreements; formal leadership selection (a combination of elections and "hand-picked" recommendations).

- **Affinity Group Leadership** Well trained in leadership and diversity and focused on results, executives across identity groups should be active, and strong and support relationships with advisors as well as share best practices and create an active connection to leadership development.

- **Executive Advisors** Members of the senior leadership team should act as champions, assume a very active role and be accountable for affinity group progress/success. They should also receive an orientation to their role and the affinity group.

- **Funding** Provide annual funding tied to approval of affinity group's business plan and past performance; generally see the return on investment value.

- **Resources** Assign a dedicated resource in the Diversity Office. Provide some level of access to corporate functions, resources and facilities; corporate and diversity website highlights affinity groups, their awards and contributions.

- **Accountability** Offer continuous oversight by the Diversity Office and advisors; require annual business plan aligned with business and workforce contributions; use associated metrics/ measurements.

Strong groups have a purpose and a plan. They often give advice and counsel to the company and to the senior diversity officer. These groups prosper with adequate budgets and management advice. Most network groups are involved in professional member development activities, business partnerships and community relations. They lead other employees toward better cultural understanding.

A company should agree to standardize guidelines for all network groups in order to present baseline requirements in the application process and approval. Consistency must be established. Recognize that employees must lead this effort and form their own groups based on guidelines and company support.

Funding and Resources

Addressing budget parameters for employee networks requires formal guidelines that should be instilled as clearly articulated company policy. Business plans should be presented by these groups to help direct appropriate funds. Specific, goal-oriented agendas should be set with a funding plan. Investment should be shared in time and expense: business-related and public-relations activities sponsored by the company; volunteer efforts shared; social events sponsored by the membership.

Many network groups are financially supported by their corporations. Although employee network budgets appear quite limited, they often partner with operational departments, thus expanding their budgetary resources. The human resources department often assists with training and recruiting resources, while the marketing, community relations, and public relations departments are targets for marketing and related activities.

In starting an employee resource group, funding must be a priority. Getting the backing of an executive sponsor will help get you get the resources needed to start. Ideally, you should choose a senior executive that reports directly to the CEO who can relay the requests.

Out & Equal surveyed ERG members from a vast array of industries and professions across the country. Seventy percent of the groups polled were larger than 50 members, and 83 percent were located in multiple sites nationally and internationally. In light of this, budgets were highly recognized, with eighty-four percent reporting having one, with the majority of the funding coming directly from the HR/Diversity Department. The annual average for employee resource groups ranged between $10,000 and $20,000, but the largest range was from in the hundreds to the high hundreds of thousands. Considering groups studied were within large companies, budgets highly depended on programs and business development participation they had.

In addition to funding, corporations often provide many other resources to their employee resource groups. In addition to needed financial support, they provide human resources to guide, support, and educate the network.

Developing a Charter

To formally initiate the development process, the employee group should seek the support of influential individuals throughout the organization. During this stage, it is important that the group develops a charter and mission statement depicting its primary goals. Committees typically begin to form, followed by elected officers.

Affinity groups should maintain a charter to outline not only the purpose of the group, but also the regulations and functional responsibilities of its members within the organization. The charter should outline the activities the group will participate in, such as create an inclusive environment, representing a shared voice, promoting a respectful workplace environment and promoting diversity initiatives.

Membership should be voluntary and open to any regularly scheduled full- or part-time employee. This section of the charter should also outline what membership provides employees, the roles and responsibilities of members, and leadership, and needs for budget considerations. An application process for groups and members should be outlined before taking on these initiatives.

Mission and Vision

One of the first demonstrated actions of any network and affinity group is mission development, or identity definition. There are clear steps towards developing an effective, clear, attainable mission. Begin with defining your story, both the company's and the group's. That story should create a sense of urgency and consist of the history of your constituency at the company. Positive stories—like executive representation and involvement, employee impact, community involvement, and targeted marketing—generate pride. Negative stories—like a lack of representation at the executive level, community missteps, negative reputation, or difficulty recruiting and/or retaining employees—highlight the need for change.

After defining the group's story, begin to define and analyze the business. Ask questions like:

- Who is the company trying to reach? Market to? Employ? Retain?

- Where do group members think the missed opportunities are?

- Given these market and business realities, how can we engage as problem-solvers and resources?

- What could we provide that is critical to the business? Short-term? Long-term? What unique, transformational role can we play?

Once these questions have answers, turn the focus inward. Evaluate the strengths, weaknesses, opportunities, and threats to the group's success. Brainstorm stakeholders and possible activities. Finally, determine a vision and mission statement with all of the above in mind.

Examples of Purpose Statements:

- "The Latino Resource Group helps improve the company's marketing efforts aimed at the fast-growing Latino population in the US, aids recruitment and retention of Latinos, promotes cultural awareness, and provides opportunities for personal and career development."

- "The Women's Leadership Network seeks to make a difference for the company by researching and recommending solutions to issues affecting women; raising the visibility of women; providing opportunities for women to develop leadership skills and broaden their network; and reaching out to women, students and teens in our community."

- "People Like Us (PLUS) serves as a network and a resource for gay, lesbian, bisexual and transgender (GLBT) employees, fosters general awareness of the comGLBT employees and their contributions, and serves as an advisor to Human Resources and Management."

- "To provide information on the needs of the disabled for internal and external customers, and supporting mobility motoring in the United States and Europe to create the vehicle of choice for customers with disabilities."

- "Assisting the company in becoming a worldwide leader in promoting religious tolerance, corporate integrity, and human dignity by helping increase and maintain religious diversity; attract, develop and retain talented employees of faith; and be more aware of religious consumers' and investors' needs."

Programs

Part of an affinity group's business plan should involve a calendar of activities and programs to be coordinated within a two-year outlook. The affinity groups and the company offer training and education. The curricula vary but the training and education prove essential. Also, the business plan should help determine roles in recruiting, mentoring, new employee engagement and sponsorship, community outreach, and representation of the company.

Social and activist programs are both important to consider. Community activities, such as food drives, tutoring, and charity walks are good programs to keep groups in-tune with the community, as well as reaching out to universities. Within the company, promoting education and developing recruiting strategies are both highly effective. Providing materials, such as writing articles or newsletters or participating in celebrations, help get companywide recognition and involvement.

The activities undertaken by employee network groups may include:

- Formal and informal training and mentoring

- Employee networking across institutional departments

- Community outreach

- Recruiting

- Assistance on marketing products and services to diversity markets

As part of these programs, one important internal function affinity groups can service is as a forum to articulate otherwise unexpressed barriers or opportunities to the employer. Bringing these faults to attention can lead to participation for the first time in events that promote these issues. Participating in community events can help extend the company name through outreach and networking. This may also assist in recruiting.

For example, Citigroup Inc. sponsored more than 45 programs in the United States that aligned with heritage months in 2006 designed by employee network groups. They helped spread knowledge about multicultural groups within the company. These network groups also developed Diversity Week, which involves lectures on diversity topics and presentations by various organizations, including the business case for diversity, LGBT issues in the workplace, age awareness, women, individuals with disabilities, and more. More than 1,000 employees participate in the programs offered.

Communications and Visibility

Regular employee communications remind employees that there are corporate support networks available. As a way to create visibility and voluntarily share information about major initiatives, concerns, and recommendations with the company and community. It is also important to publish group results and demonstrate support for other affinity group efforts. Become active participants in program initiatives of the business, e.g., new product launches, achieving safety goals.

Corporations typically allow employee network groups to utilize corporate communications resources. Communications through these mediums, however, often must be approved prior to dissemination. Operation of webpages linked to the corporate site typically required approval as well.

Companies employ a variety of communication techniques to stimulate membership retention and growth such as those seen below:

- **Event Promotion** Ensure employees are aware of special events, conferences, and activities the network sponsors.

- **Newsletters** Encourage participation in membership drives.

- **Personal Networks** Communications and relationships of existing members can help stimulate new membership and recognition of the network.

- **Website** Maintain an up-to-date website provides employees, prospective employees, and other stakeholders with information about the network, its activities, and its agenda.

- **Branding** Use brand communications to build recognition. This will link the network and the corporation to the network mission and philosophy and increases employee awareness of the existence of the network.

- **Recruitment and retention** Ensure that recruits, new employees, and existing employees receive information about all employee network groups. Send reminders.

Infrastructure

Most employee networks are self-started and organized. Employee groups usually have a diversity staff leader and a coordinating council that meet and report to the CEO. In best-practices companies, the group reports at least once every six months, and leading companies take an active interest in their network and affinity groups. These companies provide speakers and sponsorships, ask the networks to assist with recruiting and retention, and even ask them to help build market share.

Employee resource groups are traditionally organized and chartered by employees. The following are typical structural characteristics:

- Employee network groups typically consist of employees who voluntarily join together in support of the corporation's diversity policy, vision, and values.

- Employee networks offer a forum where employees can discuss issues and gain a sense of support and community.

- Employee network groups often act as a corporate business partner, offering diverse perspectives and corporate support.

Leadership should be self-generated and established. The selection of leaders is based on the commitment to the goals and parameters of the network groups and the pertinent group under formation.

Typical structural characteristics:

- Although corporate network groups are typically employee run, they commonly attain high levels of corporate support. Senior business executives at many corporations are accountable for meeting specific diversity objectives. When the CEO is personally involved, executives make a greater commitment to network groups.

- Many employee network groups have members who serve on company diversity councils and strive to routinely keep management informed of happenings.

- Most employee network groups operate with a group of officers and a board of directors comprised of individuals from the group's membership.

- Co-chair leadership structures are sometimes developed to gain a gender balance.

- Steering committees often meet monthly.

- Advisory boards are made up of senior management. They typically meet with the employee network groups on a quarterly basis.

- Alliance companies may choose to adopt the employee network groups of their parent of create their own independent groups.

Executive Sponsors

At most corporations, employee networks are sponsored by a senior executive who is able to guide the group, transmit views to the executive level, and help secure internal political and financial support for the organization. Executive management leaders drive communication of goals and ongoing management development typically through quarterly business meetings. Just as importantly, executive management reaches the management vertically, bringing acknowledgement, cooperation, and attitudinal change.

Larger groups typically an executive champion who may report directly to the CEO, Senior Vice President, Board of Directors, and/or the Diversity Office. These executive sponsors are the direct messengers to senior management. Additionally, employee network groups typically partner with the human resources and diversity departments in order to stay connected with the company happenings as well as other employee resource groups.

Monitoring and Measuring

Today there is a strong need to portray value throughout all workplace initiatives. Employee network groups are no exception. To gain access to corporate funding, benefits and positive impact on return on investment need to be demonstrated. As network membership levels continue to grow and the need for funding increases, network leaders will seek ways to quantify value and return on investment.

The ultimate goal is to have tools available that efficiently measure the effectiveness of employee network groups in reaching membership and corporate objectives such as diversity recruitment and inclusion, employee satisfaction, corporate reputation, and sales generation.

The Difficulty with Measurement

The effects of employee network groups on corporate objectives are sometimes difficult to measure. If companies want to measure the effect on diversity sales, for example, they may utilize measurements based upon sales, incremental revenues, and overall profitability throughout new market segments. Knowledgeable professionals understand, however, that these measurements cannot be directly attributed to the efforts of employee network groups alone. Judgment is oftentimes required, leading to varying levels of subjectivity. Unlike most other business initiatives, evaluating diversity initiatives and quantifying their results have proven to be uniquely challenging.

Why are the effects of employee resource groups hard to measure?

- Endeavors are fragmented across business units, functions, and departments.

- In some companies, these networks are relatively new initiatives.

- Both tangible and intangible benefits exist.

- Judgment is often required because the results of most of the measure employed cannot be fully attributed to employee network group campaigns alone.

Measurement processes should take these considerations into account to create the most effective and accurate results. Here are some tips on how to conduct employee network group measurement and evaluations:

- **The key to setting objectives is measurability.** The corporation must establish telling standards by which the success of employee network group efforts can be measured. Without specific goals, there can be no gauge as to the presence of progress.

- **Measurement techniques vary based upon objectives of the endeavor.** Employee network groups are typically assumed to aid in diversity efforts and strengthen the bond between corporation and employee. These groups are not typically created to sell products. The problem with measurement is that its scope is limited. Oftentimes employee resource groups do not produce instant gratification in the form of monetary reward to the corporation. Results often come after lengthy periods of time. Corporations should ensure that this is taken into account.

- **Include stakeholders in measurement.** Effective corporate decision-makers include their stakeholders throughout the measurement process. As a best practice, successful corporations understand that stakeholder opinion should be monitored throughout the entire employee network group funding process. Once key stakeholder confidence is established, corporations can proceed with confidence with the knowledge that their investments are worthwhile.

- **Measurement techniques depend upon corporate objectives.** The value of distinct measurement tools are dependent upon the unique circumstances of each company, including how the company rates specified objectives and aligns results based upon those goals. For example, if the company's primary objective is to increase diversity recruitment and retention, they should engage in measurements that monitor changes in these areas. Conversely, if the organization's primary goal is to drive diversity sales, then they would employee measurement tools that gauge changes in sales transactions throughout the target market area. Regular assessments are imperative.

- **Regular measurement and assessments will allow both the corporation and the employee network group to measure their respective benefits received.** For example, employees may be most concerned with satisfying career and work/life balance, while corporations desire the benefit of creating motivated employees willing to advance in their careers, learn new skills, and maintain a relationship with the company.

Measuring Diversity and Inclusion Initiatives

The most common measurements sought by employee resource groups are their effects upon the overall corporate diversity initiative. The list of functions that follows may be utilized as a guide for organizations as they strive to be best in class.

The functions of diversity and inclusion include:

- Recruitment and retention

- Work/life

- Purchasing and supplier diversity communications, media, marketing, and advertising

- Customer and client relations

- Community relations

- Events and sponsorships

- Third party relationships/strategic alliances

- Public policy and government relations

As a best practice, affinity groups should establish measurement processes to assess their impact upon these functional diversity areas. These results can then be measured and benchmarked against other corporate network groups.

Measurement Tools

The following table provides a sampling of common employee network group objectives and offers examples of measurement barometers for each.

Objectives	Barometer
Enhance employee morale	Monitor productivity levels; survey for morale; measure employee participation levels
Diversity recruitment and retention	Measure minority recruitment and retention throughout decided periods; benchmark numbers against past results; survey minority employees for satisfaction levels; monitor retention and reasons for employee resignations; compare statistics for network members versus non-members
Employee networking	Track networking opportunities; survey membership regarding this subject and acquire need for improvements
Employee education	Survey employee following seminars and speaker series to determine their level of learning and satisfaction; monitor the number of educational opportunities provided; benchmark opportunities against other networks both internal and external to the company.
Enhance minority leadership and representation	Monitor leadership positions held by minorities; compare these numbers to past statistics and benchmark against others throughout the industry
Diversity sales activation	Calculate new sales for targeted market; calculate changes in incremental revenues; match sales data against periods without employee resource group support
Diversity sales retention	Monitor overall profitability and incremental revenues throughout periods; compare for markets not supported by employee resource groups
Increase awareness about the employee resource group and its objectives	Conduct regular surveys; hold sessions without control groups to assess awareness levels
Target marketing	Survey attendance and demographics of attendees throughout regular intervals of the event; compare pre- and post-event sales or sales of prior years
Enhance/alter corporate image	Conduct surveys throughout multiple periods such as quarterly or biannually to consumers, employees and constituents
Media mentions	Calculate media mentions and awards
Message promotion	Survey awareness levels both internal and external to company
Enhance community relations	Measure community benefits; engage community constituents to provide feedback

Conclusion

In this chapter, we:

• Investigated the benefits of employee network and affinity groups to the company and employees.

• Considered the impact of employee network and affinity groups on recruitment, retention, and leadership and product development.

• Reviewed the basics of employee network and affinity group operations, to include mission and vision, charters, funding and resources, programs, and visibility.

• Analyzed the typical infrastructure of employee network and affinity groups.

• Examined the benefits, challenges, and tools of measuring the impact of employee network and affinity groups on the bottom line.

Corporations increasingly understand that employee network and affinity groups provide many positive benefits not only to the company and its employees, but also to the community, business partners, shareholders, and other stakeholder groups, as well. Leading companies recognize that these important groups have passed the point of being merely a social function and utilize these groups as business partners for the sectors they represent through marketing, employee support, and product testing.

Executives should develop relationships with these employee resource groups and view them as business partners for not only marketing campaigns and product development, but also for the search for talent. Leveraging affinity groups in this way will increase corporations' bottom lines and help develop a highly successful, inclusive work environment.

For more on network and affinity groups, visit diversitybestpractices.com for the Network & Affinity Leadership Handbook or to learn more about the annual Network & Affinity Leadership Congress (NALC).

Corporate Examples

Abbott Laboratories

Employee networks play a vital role in building an inclusive culture at Abbott. By focusing on career development, mentoring, informal networking and work-life management, our networks expand opportunities for women and minorities to advance into leadership roles. Networks are sponsored by corporate officers, who help align the group's objectives with Abbott's business strategy. Nearly 8,000 U.S. employees participate in leadership networks. These include:

- LA VOICE Network (Hispanic/Latino),
- Women Leaders in Action
- Black Business Network
- Asian Cultural Leadership Network
- PRIDE Network (gay/ lesbian)
- Part-Time Network

American Express

Employee networks sponsor programs that enhance professional and personal growth. Participants engage in educational activities, including job fairs and cultural events; act as liaisons to management and to the community; participate in outreach and volunteer programs; support employee recruitment and retention initiatives; and enhance marketing efforts in targeted communities. Participation in networks also offers employees a supportive environment in which to expand their skills and develop leadership capabilities.

- AHORA – Hispanic Network
- SPIN – Hispanic Network
- ASIA and EWEX Exchange – Asian Employee Network
- BEN – Black Employee Network
- CHAI – Jewish Employee Network
- DAN – Disabilities Awareness Network
- PRIDE – Lesbian, Gay, Bisexual, Transgender Employee Network
- NAIP – Native American Employee Network
- Nation – Native American Employee Network

- Passages – Employees Over 40 Network

- SALT – Christian Employee Network

- WIN – Women's Interest Network

Amgen, Inc.

Amgen embraces a culture of inclusion in many ways, including a strong commitment to equal opportunity and affirmative action as well as over 25 company sponsored affinity group and diversity council chapters that engage in expanding inclusion strategies, business acumen and career development opportunities for all Amgen staff. With the goals to engage, develop and retain staff, these groups provide mentoring and networking opportunities as well as develop and strengthen community partnerships with local and nationwide organizations. More than 2,500 staff members participate in affinity groups at Amgen, which currently include:

- Amgen Asian Association (AAA)

- Amgen Black Employees Network (ABEN)

- Amgen DisAbled Employees Network (ABLE)

- Amgen Diversity Councils (ADC)

- Amgen International Network (AIN)

- Amgen Indian Subcontinent Network (AISN)

- Amgen Latin Employees Network (ALEN)

- Amgen Middle Eastern Employees Network (AMEEN)

- Amgen Network for Gay and Lesbian Employees (ANGLE)

- Amgen Women's Interactive Network (AWIN)

- Diversity Councils

Applied Materials

Applied Materials offers employees the opportunity to participate in affinity groups, which are voluntary, employee-driven groups organized around a particular shared interest or dimension. Affinity group members may have a common cultural history and perspective, yet, each affinity group takes a unique approach to addressing the specific needs of its membership. Each group works to create an open forum for idea exchange and to strengthen the linkage to and within diverse communities in support of Applied Materials' business objectives.

In addition to supporting the company and community as a whole, affinity groups provide services to their members that enhance individual effectiveness and job satisfaction through networking and professional development. All affinity groups are open to all employees at Applied Materials.

AT&T

AT&T has several Employee Resource Groups (ERGs) that are open to all employees and reflect the diversity of the company's employee base. AT&T's Employee Resource Groups support the company's commitment to diversity and inclusion through their efforts in the workplace, the marketplace, and the community. AT&T recognizes the value and goodwill that these groups can provide in furthering the company's goal, values and interests. Employee resource groups include representation for women, African-Americans, Asian-Americans, Hispanics/Latinos, Native Americans, GLBT, veterans and employees with disabilities.

- Women

- African-Americans

- Asian-Americans

- Hispanics/Latinos

- Native Americans

- LEAGUE (GLBT)

- Veterans

- Employees with disabilities

Cisco Systems, Inc.

Cisco values and fosters diversity, development, and growth opportunities for staff through employee networks. These networks join employees to help reinforce the value of all aspects of each member's personality. Valuing the differences in each person increases individual and team performance, productivity, and satisfaction. Cisco believes that its employee networks are critical to an inclusive organizational culture.

- Women's Action Networks

- Cisco Black Employee Network (CBEN)

- Conexion, the Cisco Latino Network

- Gay Lesbian Bisexual Transgender (GLBT) and Advocates

- Cisco Asian Affinity Network (CAAN)

- Indians Connected

Clorox Company

To help diverse employees connect with one another and collectively with the company, Clorox sponsors five employee resource groups: African American, Asian/Pacific, Hispanic, GLBT and Women. Each group is sponsored by a member of the Clorox Executive Committee and led by a vice president of the company.

- African American
- Asian/Pacific
- Hispanic
- GLBT
- Women

Colgate-Palmolive Company

Colgate's commitment to diversity and inclusion includes employee network groups, community support, and support for local educational institutions. Colgate supports community groups and organizations, which promote the development and advancement of women and diverse groups in the workforce.

- Asian American Group (AAG)
- Asian Heritage Group (AHG)
- Black Action Committee (BAC)
- Diversity Councils
- Hispanic Action Network (HAN)
- Women's Network

Dell, Inc.

Dell sponsors a community of networking groups formed by employees with common interests in areas such as ethnicity, gender, nationality, lifestyle, and sexual orientation. These groups offer Dell employees the opportunity to network with other employees from around the company, while providing encouragement and an enhanced sense of belonging through informal mentoring, professional and community events and access to personal and professional development and growth. Additionally, networking groups help foster a more inclusive work environment, improve communication among employees and enhance understanding of all employees about the value of diversity.

- BRIDGE - Building Relationships in Diverse Group Environments (African-American Networking Group)
- W.I.S.E. - Women In Search of Excellence

- aDellante - Hispanic Networking Group

- PRIDE - Partnering for Respect of Individuality in the Dell Environment (A Gay, Lesbian, Bisexual, Transgender & Straight Alliance)

- A.I.M. - Asians in Motion

Deloitte & Touche USA LLP

Programs sponsored by seven business resource groups and more than 80 local chapters last year encouraged our professionals to forge effective networks with colleagues inside and outside the organization. These events also helped us recruit top talent, win new business, and grow existing relationships.

- Asian BRG (ABRG)

- Black Employee Network (BEN)

- Deloitte Parents' Network (DPN)

- Gay, Lesbian, Bisexual, Transgender and Allies (GLOBE)

- Hispanic/Latino(a) Network (HNet)

- International BRG (IBRG)

- Women's Initiative (WIN)

In many instances, the early efforts of local BRGs have begun to pay sustainable dividends. The effect can be seen on our bottom line in terms of the acquisition of new business and new talent.

McDonald's Corporation

Women's Leadership Network, Asian Employee Network, McDonald's African American Council, Hispanic Employee Network, Gays, Lesbians and Allies at McDonald's and others provide McDonald's employees with career development, advocacy, support, recruitment and retention assistance. These employee networks also help the company achieve its diversity vision by: improving process like performance feedback and employee development; recruitment and retaining excellent employees; maintaining a better connection with our diverse customer base.

- Women's Leadership Network

- Asian Employee Network

- McDonald's African American Council

- Hispanic Employee Network

- Gays, Lesbians and Allies at McDonald's

The McGraw Hill Companies, Inc.

Through grassroots-driven Employee Resource Groups (ERGs) and business-focused Diversity Councils, we recognize and support diversity in the workplace. The Hispanic Heritage Network (HHN), Women's Initiative for Networking and Success (WINS), Black Employees at McGraw-Hill (BEAM), and the Gay, Lesbian, Bisexual and Transgender (GLBT) Employee Resource Group enable employees to connect and discuss a shared set of interests, experiences and perspectives.

ERGs have also been vital in fostering a mentoring culture throughout The McGraw-Hill Companies — the McGraw-Hill Mentoring Program was conceived of and piloted through WINS and HHN has recently launched a mentoring program focused on serving the needs of our Hispanic employees.

- Hispanic Heritage Network (HHN)
- Women's Initiative for Networking and Success (WINS)
- Black Employees at McGraw-Hill (BEAM)
- Gay, Lesbian, Bisexual and Transgender (GLBT)

Motorola

Motorola's diversity councils help integrate inclusion into its marketing, community involvement, recruitment and employee development initiatives. Led by senior executives and open to any Motorola employee, the councils sponsor inclusion events, collaborate with external inclusion organizations, raise awareness and mentor employees. Our councils include:

- Asian Business Council — United States
- Black Business Council — United States
- Gay, Lesbian, Bisexual and Transgender Business Council — United States
- Latino Business Council — United States
- People with Disabilities Business Council — United States
- Women's Business Council — Canada, China, India, Japan, Korea, Malaysia, Singapore, United States and Europe, Middle East and Africa region
- State Diversity Councils (United States) — Arizona, Florida
- Country/Region Diversity Councils — Columbia, Central America, Mexico, Peru, Puerto Rico, South Africa, Venezuela
- Business/Function Diversity Councils (Global) — Home & Networks Mobility, Law, Enterprise Mobility, Technology

State Farm Insurance Company

State Farm recognizes that employees have long met informally to network, mentor each other, develop professionally, and assist the Company in various ways. Our policy allows employee groups to meet more formally and seek recognition as State Farm Employee Resource Groups.

At State Farm, Employee Resource Groups are committed to serving as a resource in the areas of employee growth and development, recruitment, and retention to help us meet current and future needs for a more diverse customer base and employee workforce.

Any State Farm employee who supports the Group's business purpose is welcome to join and do not need to be a member of the demographic segment the group is formed around in order to participate.

We currently recognize Employee Resource Groups formed around the following demographic segments:

- African American/Black
- Asian
- Gays/Lesbians/Bisexuals/Transgender
- Hispanic/Latino/Latina
- Military/Public Service in Canada
- Men
- Parents/Families
- People with Disabilities
- Women
- Young Adult

Sun Microsystems, Inc.

An Employee Resource Group is a network of Sun employees who share a common identity, characteristic, or set of interests. Employee Resource Groups exist for the betterment of Sun, engaging themselves in initiatives and activities which contribute towards Sun's success and which insure a work environment in which each candidate, employee, and customer is treated with respect, dignity, fairness, and cultural sensitivity.

The efforts of Sun's Employee Resource Groups complement Global Inclusion's focus areas of Attracting and Retaining diverse top talent and the Attraction and Retention of a diverse global customer base.

Interested employees voluntarily subscribe to Employee Resource Groups through established online aliases. These aliases, open to all interested employees, provide members with opportunity to exchange information and ideas, network with those sharing similar interests, and plan sponsored activities.

Employee Resource Groups:

- Asian American Diversity Network (AADN)
- Black Employee Network (BEN)
- Gays, Lesbians, and Friends (GLAF)
- Society of Latinos (SOL)
- SunWomen
- Legal Diversity Council
- Interns @ Sun
- Global Inclusion Community

Walmart

The Associate Resource Groups are committed to advancing our business by leveraging the diversity of our associates to become and employer and retailer of choice in the communities we serve, and by providing advice on culturally appropriate products and advertising.

The Associate Resource Groups are open to all associates at the Corporate Office and they include:

- Asian Pacific Islander Associate Resource Group (API)
- Hispanic Latino Associate Resource Group (HLARG)
- Leading and Empowering Associates with Disabilities Associate Resource Group (LEAD)
- Lesbian, Gay, Bisexual & Transgender Associate Resource Group (PRIDE)
- American Indian and Alaskan Native Associate Resource Group (Tribal Voices)
- African American Associate Resource Group (UNITY)
- Women's Resource Council (WRC)

Currently, there are more than 2,000 associates participating in the Groups at our Corporate Office, and 30 corporate officers serve as executive sponsors by providing counsel, advice and support to members.

Associate Resource Groups are making a difference in the way we do business by focusing on the following objectives:

- Diversity best practices insight

- Business support

- Associate Development

- Community Involvement

- Recruitment and retention

Weyerhaeuser Company

Diversity Business Networks are employee resource groups that create a sense of belonging for employees and assist with recruitment, retention, work climate, and a culture of diverse talent. Our current groups include:

- ACCESS

- Community Overcoming Labels, Opening Minds & Reducing Stereotypes (COLORS/ GLBTQ)

- Generation Next (Gen Nex)

- Hispanic Opportunities for Leadership Achievement (HOLA)

- Weyerhaeuser Black Employee Alliance (WBEA)

- Women in Action

Xerox Corporation

Independent employee caucus groups play an important role at Xerox, advocating self-development, openness, equal opportunity and inclusion for the entire Xerox community. Groups representing Women, Blacks, Hispanics, Asians, and Gay, Lesbian , Bisexual, and Transgender employees provide members with an avenue to improve society via their activities and success.

- Black Women's Leadership Council (BWLC)

- Gay, Lesbian, Bisexual, and Transgender Employees (Galaxe Pride at Work)

- Hispanic Association for Professional Advancement (HAPA)

- National Black Employee Association (NBEA)

- The Women's Alliance (TWA)

- Asians Coming Together (ACT)

Case Study: ConAgra Foods

At ConAgra Foods, Employee Resource Networks (ERNs) are the key ingredient in the recipe for creating a diverse and inclusive culture. In just two years, ERN participation has grown from 200 members in four networks to more than 1,200 active participants in six networks across the United States. The catalyst for growth is the result of a 2007 strategic planning process which brought together a cross-functional team of employees to map out the company's first ever, comprehensive strategy for Diversity and Inclusion.

Using the new strategic plan as the foundation, there was clear opportunity for ConAgra to relaunch existing ERNs and expand the networks to align with the company's strategic objective to nourish its people in order to attract, retain, and engage its employee base. To enable the ERNs to impact the transition in culture, specially designed charters outline the opportunity to further advance company strategy and include initiatives to accelerate innovation in product development and human capital processes, build teams of external advocates for recruiting and community outreach, and develop members both personally and professionally. ConAgra Foods' current ERNs include the ConAgra Asian Network, ConAgra Black Employee Network, ConAgra Latino Network, Illuminations (Lesbian, Gay, Bisexual, Transgender, and Allies), Young Professionals Network, and the Women's Leadership Council (WLC).

Neighborhood Approach

A primary challenge of the ERN relaunch was to expand the benefits of the network to employees outside of the Omaha, Neb. headquarters location, while maintaining a consistent, operational structure. The concept was to charter each network as a single community made up of neighborhood locations. For example, WLC neighborhoods include Omaha, Naperville, Ill., Edina, Minn., Kennewick, Wash., and Field Sales. The WLC network lead is mentored by a senior executive on the CEO's leadership team and each neighborhood leader receives additional support from a network member at the vice president level. This neighborhood approach is very effective in connecting women across the organization, while meeting regional and functional needs. To facilitate the sharing and planning of events and monitor initiative progress, neighborhood leaders conduct monthly conference calls, manage a Microsoft SharePoint site on the employee intranet, and host development webinars.

Emerging Leaders

ERN members work together to provide unique insights to engage a diverse work force and create products to reach an ever-changing consumer base. Each year, they choose projects that tie directly to a business priority and are given the opportunity to report and present their results to senior leaders. As a result, the neighborhood and project lead roles are highly sought after by network members because of the skill development and visibility opportunities. In addition, the network sponsor, executive vice president of Human Resources, and vice president of Diversity and Inclusion meet annually to discuss viable candidates for ERN leadership positions as a part of the talent management process. In 2009, to proactively develop employees who volunteer for and accept the ERN leadership challenge, the organization launched a full-day Leadership and Learning Lab as one of ConAgra Foods' signature leadership development programs.

Case Study: Ernst & Young

As one of the Big Four auditors, Ernst & Young knows how to treat its global clients, catering to unique cultural needs and providing vast professional services. But with a diverse employee population of more than 130,000, catering to their needs and providing services can seem like a daunting task. In an effort to provide top-level support and service to employees and clients alike, Ernst & Young has discovered the value and importance of internal network and affinity groups.

Between 1995 and 2005, there was a 79 percent rise of minority employees at Ernst & Young. With that number continuing to increase, inclusion is a high priority. "Inclusiveness is embedded in our culture," said Petty Homan, an audit manager from Chicago. "We're very proactive in creating and supporting affinity groups," or People Resource Networks (PRN), as they are called at Ernst & Young.

At E&Y, PRNs are specifically designed to give members of minority groups a setting to connect with professionals with similar backgrounds, ask questions, exchange information, and share experiences. The largest PRNs are the ethnic groups: African American, Hispanic, and Asian Pacific Islander. These provide vast opportunities for local minorities to network with their peers and colleagues through activities with each other and the community. Ernst & Young encourages members to become involved with external organizations such as the National Association of Black Accountants, the Association of Latino Professional in Finance and Accounting, and the National Asian American Society of Accountants. This fosters personal and communal growth and development.

While the ethnic PRNs are the largest, they were not the first. bEYond was formed years ago as a network for lesbian, gay, bisexual and transgender people. Ernst & Young frequently ranks in the top ten lists for GLBT-friendly companies. The affinity group bEYond works to rid the organization of discrimination due to gender identity/expression. Its greatest success came when Ernst & Young was the first of the Big Four to score a 100% rating on the Human Rights Campaign equality index. bEYond has active chapters in almost all of the major cities in the U.S. and Canada.

Ernst & Young is also a pioneer for inclusion and rights of workers with disabilities. The PRN AccessAbilities raises awareness about disability issues in the workplace while providing guidance for those affected. AccessAbilities also holds frequent conference calls as a forum to discuss how the firm can improve its support of people with disabilities. The Abilities Champion Network strives to ensure that the message of disability-awareness is included in all communications, meetings, and events. Ernst & Young also offers a unique Network for Parents of Children with Special Health Care Needs that allows parents to connect with each other and with outside professionals for advice and support. Not only does this network hold confidential monthly calls, it also sponsors six condition-specific subgroups.

Parents also have networks and PRNs within Ernst & Young. My JournEY was created over 10 years ago as a sponsor of programs and resources specifically for working parents, both men and women. More recently, it has organized and created the Working Moms Network, a support system that promotes connectivity, networking, and mentoring opportunities for all mothers. Almost 2,000 women and men participated in its launch conference call in 2006. Area groups meet quarterly to discuss topics, share best practices, and advise each other on being working parents. My JournEY also includes the Working Dads Network, a full lactation program, concierge services, and back-up child and adult care.

Beyond that, women at Ernst & Young have multiple resources for their growth and development. PLAN is a network that provides mentoring opportunities with Executive Board members. ACCESS connects women who are actively pursuing positions of partnership or leadership. Professional Women's Networks, and a variety of subnetworks, work internally and externally to raise the status of women in the business and auditing world.

Overall, employees at Ernst & Young feel valued and connected with the large presence of networks and affinity groups. These programs foster communication within a minority group while providing an excellent means for feedback to senior management about diversity strategies.

Case Study: General Electric

Ranked by Forbes as the world's largest company, General Electric began its diversity initiative as a U.S.-based program but has since grown it to encompass the company's global efforts. Deborah Elam, the company's chief diversity officer, shares that GE's diversity initiative is integral to the company's success. "No matter where we [General Electric] work or do business, we want to attract and retain the very best talent," she said.

As part of the company's diversity initiative, GE's employee network groups are critical to the company's diversity mission and aid it in attracting, retaining, and developing the best talent. General Electric operates six network groups: the African American Forum, the Women's Network, the Hispanic Forum, the Asian-Pacific Forum, the GLBT Forum, and the Native American Forum.

Each of the network groups offer mentoring, coaching, and networking opportunities and help to create opportunities that allow for interaction between the network group members and GE senior executives. The company reports that more than 20,000 women participate in the Women's Network programs.

Additionally, GE's African American Forum and Women's Network both have active chapters for employees based outside of the United States as offered many of the same programs abroad that it offers here.

The company's network groups began as volunteer, grassroots efforts and were primarily used as network and social opportunities for company employees. These groups now aid group members by helping them develop the attributes they will need to further their careers within the organization. The network groups also each follow four basic steps that are considered vital: develop your vision, get buy-in from senior executive leadership, appoint a national champion, and develop a business plan.

"At General Electric, our diversity initiatives are not just 'flavor of the month.' They are a part of every general manager's measurements. And our diverse workforce is really part of our culture and part of our success. It's who we are, it's constant," said Steve Canale, manager of recruiting and staffing services for General Electric.

Tamla Oates-Forney, program manager for GE's "Global Employer of Choice" initiative explained that each of the company's minority network groups aid the company in "assimilating cultures and recruiting, orientation, career development, promotion, retention and more." Forney noted that newly hired women and minorities at GE are put in touch with appropriate groups when they start and the groups pair them with mentors.

General Electric leaders from each of the company's different business offerings serve as advisors to the network groups, and CEO Jeffrey Immelt also shares in the experience.

GE's network groups raise scholarship money, and the GE Fund provides more money through a matching gifts program. The GE Fund also gives grants to help underwrite middle and high school students from diverse backgrounds to get them interested and help them get ready for college-level math and science.

"We'll have African American female leaders and corporate executives serve as mentors and conference speakers," Oates-Forney said. "It shows that we are interested in bringing in diverse people at the entry level, and we want to continue to grow them and keep them within the corporation." All of these efforts are part of GE's commitment to become the global employer of choice.

Chapter 11

Supplier Diversity

Supplier diversity is an area of expanding interest for corporate America, non-profits, and the government. Corporations are setting ambitious goals for themselves to reach out to businesses not traditionally included to a large extent in the supply chain. Gaining executive commitment from the CEO and others in leadership is essential for the success of the overall supplier diversity program, and as a result, CEO and executive interest, as well as Board review of supplier goals, have increased significantly in the past decade.

Many corporations spend millions—even billions—of dollars a year on goods and services. Yet historically, women-owned business enterprises (WBEs) and minority-owned business enterprises (MBEs) have been left behind in terms of securing supplier contracts with large organizations. In response, supplier diversity programs have sprung up in companies of all industries and areas, and today, some companies are going beyond MBEs and WBEs by also considering LGBT-owned business and veteran-owned businesses in their procurement process. Although many of these programs were formed to promote a positive public image, many corporations are now realizing that maintaining diverse suppliers can also help the company improve its bottom line in countless ways.

Additionally, government and nonprofit groups are increasingly monitoring the percentage and of contracts awarded to minority- and women-owned firms. U.S. laws give corporations major incentives to use small business suppliers when contracting with US federal, state, or public agencies. Large businesses also must administer a "subcontracting plan" that specifies activities related to small business suppliers. And in some instances, the sub-tier large business suppliers of a prime contractor may also need to have such a plan.

In most cases, the supplier diversity function reports to the vice president of purchasing with a dotted line to the senior diversity officer and/or executive diversity council. But as more diversity officers report at a higher level, and not through HR, many of the companies have the function reporting directly to the diversity and inclusion officer.

In this chapter, we will explore the following questions:

• What are the current trends in supplier diversity?

• How should companies report supplier diversity progress? What should be included on a supplier diversity checklist?

• What are some corporate examples of supplier diversity goals and achievements?

Increasing Pressure for Supplier Diversity

For most companies, the commitment to minority- and women-owned business purchasing is goal-focused and measured. Pressure for more supplier diversity initially may have been created by affirmative action or other suits; however, most companies now see the positive side. Small business, women, and minorities are their markets and communities, and government contractors, for one, know the importance of supplier diversity as a differentiator to winning contracts.

Companies often have large staffs, large budgets, and large dollar amounts devoted to supplier diversity. For example, roughly 97% of the Fortune 500 companies set percentage or dollar goals on supplier diversity.

Staffing for supplier diversity is growing, with an average of approximately two to three individuals assigned to the function. Sometimes as many as 10-15 people are assigned to support supplier diversity throughout the company. As budgets have increased so has personnel, programs, advertising and marketing, training, conferences, and seminars.

Additionally, government and nonprofit groups are increasingly monitoring the percentage and size of contracts awarded to minority- and women-owned firms.

Approximately 80% of executive Diversity Councils and CEOs at U.S. corporations with supplier diversity programs are involved in setting the policies and goals for purchasing diversity. This high-level leadership makes a difference. According to a new survey by the Women's Business Enterprise National Council, 93% of companies with active CEO involvement maintain a list or database of women-owned business enterprise (WBE) and/ or minority-owned business enterprise (MBE) suppliers. Ninety-one percent (91%) have a written company policy that specifically includes WBE/MBEs.

In the meantime, support programs are expanding. Ancillary programs, such as mentor-protégé and training, are growing as more companies seek to help minority suppliers gain more training and access to contracts. Purchasing-based association advocates are also gaining clout. The Minority Supplier Development Council, the Women Business Enterprise National Council, the Women Business Development Council, the National Association of Women Business Owners' Women Business Owners Corporation, the Minority Business Round Table, and the Latin American Management Association, among others, are gaining influence with corporations.

But as more money is spent with suppliers, pressure will increase as interest groups send report cards to corporate CEOs, diversity councils, and Boards. The government and media pay attention to supplier diversity programs, and awards and recognition in this area are on the rise. The following page offers a basic checklist to consider when beginning to track the effectiveness of your company's supplier diversity program.

Reporting on Supplier Diversity – A Sample Checklist

Total Dollars Per Year

✓ Dollars spent last year

✓ Percentage of total procurement

Executive Support

✓ CEO

✓ Executive Diversity Council

✓ Board of Directors

Structure and Staffing

✓ Provide the staff leadership

✓ Provide the structural support

Communicate the Goals and Results

✓ Publish the goals and results

✓ Use internal and external publications as well as the Internet

✓ Highlight some of your suppliers

Ensure Accountability for Meeting or Exceeding the Supplier Diversity Goals

✓ Measure results

✓ Award performance

✓ Penalize deficiencies and goals not reached

✓ Link to performance evaluations

✓ Provide periodic reports

Encourage Special Programs

✓ Matchmaking

✓ Mentoring

Conclusion

In this chapter, we:

- Examined current trends in supplier diversity.

- Considered how companies should determine supplier diversity goals.

- Shared corporate examples of supplier diversity goals and achievements.

Best-practice companies constantly evaluate vendors to find the industry experience, knowledge, and capability needed to deliver products that reflect the diversity of their customer base. A significant component of these efforts involves cultivating relationships with typically underutilized businesses, and working to incorporate these companies into their network of vendors whenever possible.

Growing a diverse supplier base only makes sense given the increasingly diverse markets that most companies serve in this global age. Partnering with a diverse range of suppliers to provide products and services that meet or exceed customer needs enables a company to serve its consumers to the best extent possible. Those companies that combine outstanding supplier diversity initiatives and outcomes with other best-in-class diversity and inclusion programs will maintain a competitive advantage, win new business, retain customers, and reinforce their brand around the world.

Corporate Examples

Bank of America

With 9 percent of Tier II procurement spent with minority- and women-owned suppliers, Bank of America has a clear connection to its multicultural communities. The bank has training/mentoring for MBEs and WBEs, provides financial assistance for them and includes supplier diversity in its RFPs.

Comerica Bank

Comerica Bank's supplier diversity is outstanding, with 14.2 percent of Tier I procurement going to minority-owned business enterprises and 11.1 percent going to women-owned business enterprises. Of Tier II, 7.3 percent goes to MBEs and 2.1 percent to WBEs.

Ford Motor Co.

Ford maintains a five-year business plan for MBE and WBE suppliers. Spend objectives are contained in the global purchasing scorecard and assessed in the CEO's biweekly business-plan review with his direct reports.

Health Care Services Corp.

Health Care Services Corp. has accelerated its supplier-diversity efforts in recent years, with 5.6 percent of Tier I procurement now going to minority-owned business enterprises and 4.6 percent to women-owned business enterprises. Of Tier II, 39 percent goes to MBEs and 42.5 percent goes to WBEs.

Henry Ford Health System

Forty-one percent of Henry Ford's philanthropy budget goes to multicultural groups, most in the Detroit area. Henry Ford also spends 7.3 percent of its Tier I procurement with minority-owned suppliers.

IBM Corp.

IBM was one of the first companies to reach out to LGBT suppliers (who are certified by the National Gay and Lesbian Chamber and Commerce). Of its Tier II procurement, 12.4 percent goes to LGBT-owned businesses. The company has excellent metrics to assess supplier-diversity success and strong relationships with external certifying organizations.

Marriott International

Marriott had already nearly doubled its goal to spend $1 billion with minority-business enterprises by 2010.

MGM MIRAGE

In 2008, MGM MIRAGE dedicated one employee to coach suppliers and obtain Tier II reporting. This included spend threshold and propensity to include diversity in the supply chain.

PG&E

PG&E spends 11.8 percent of its Tier I procurement budget with minority-owned business enterprises and 5.1 percent with women-owned business enterprises. The company audits its supplier-diversity numbers and integrates supplier diversity into its overall business strategy. In addition, PG&E has strong metrics to assess its supplier-diversity success, including: diversity as percentage of total spend; the number of diverse suppliers; revenue growth of diverse suppliers; recognitions received for supplier-diversity success from outside organizations; and savings as a result of contracting with WMBEs. The company also ties procurement-management compensation to supplier-diversity success.

Xerox Corp.

The company reports that of its Tier I (direct contractor) procurement, 13.2 percent goes to minority-owned business enterprises (MBEs), 19.3 percent goes to women-owned business enterprises (WBEs) and 0.1 percent goes to gay- and lesbian-owned business enterprises. Of its Tier II (subcontractor) procurement, 7.6 percent goes to MBEs, 6.8 percent goes to WBEs and 1 percent goes to gay- and lesbian-owned business enterprises.

Case Study: OfficeMax, Inc.

When most consumers walk in to an office supply store, they are not thinking about buying a pen or a printer purchased from a historically underutilized business (HUB). Luckily, someone is thinking about it. OfficeMax, Inc., a leader in business-to-business and retail office products, is one of the only office supply companies to receive awards for its support of minority and women-owned businesses.

OfficeMax has been leading the way in supplier diversity for over 30 years. When the company first implemented a corporate supplier diversity policy, it did so without any government or customer mandates. Moreover, OfficeMax was a founding member of the National Minority Supplier Development Council in 1972 and continues to be an active, corporate member today. In 1992, it launched its Supplier Diversity Program, the industry's first marketing program for minority- and women-owned business enterprises (MWBE) products. OfficeMax continues to be the leader in resale of office products from MWBEs. It also supports the economic development of companies owned by veterans and firms with employees who are developmentally or physically challenged (PCs).

But OfficeMax never takes credit for these products. It purchases the inventory from the MWBEs and PCs and then markets it for resale to customers and other businesses. Its catalogs clearly mark which supplies come from MWBEs and PCs. This icon also helps OfficeMax track purchasing patterns to identify any potential for increased MWBE and PC purchases. Its commitment to a diverse supplier base has paid off tangibly. At the end of 2004, OfficeMax's Supplier Diversity Program included 142 suppliers: 42 were minority-owned, 64 employed blind or severely disabled workers, and the remaining 36 were owned by women. These practices benefit OfficeMax itself as well as the suppliers and customers.

Having such diverse suppliers provides OfficeMax customers with highly competitive prices, one-stop shopping, quality products, and supplier certification. Supplier diversity also brings innovation and flexibility in to the office supply realm as small companies are more flexible than large suppliers. Suppliers also benefit from working with OfficeMax. They get nationwide sales and distribution at no cost; they have access to corporate customers usually off-limits to small suppliers; they get fast payment and flexible advertising amounts; and they receive assistance with product development. Supplying OfficeMax as a MWBE or PC provides an opportunity for unprecedented growth and expansion.

Beside the effect of having their products on shelves, OfficeMax offers further support and assistance to MWBE and PC suppliers. It sponsors scholarships for multicultural suppliers to attend Tuck School of Business at Dartmouth College. There are quarterly Webcasts with managers and business experts to promote best practices and provide coaching and mentoring.

However, there are challenges that exist with supplier diversity. It is difficult to encourage customers to abandon brand knowledge and buy products made by small or disadvantaged companies. OfficeMax is aware of this challenge and now instructs customer service representatives to push MWBE- and PC-made products as well as reminding customers of OfficeMax's continued commitment to diversity.

Maybe, with the help of employees and suppliers, customers will eventually walk in to an OfficeMax searching for a pen made by a woman-owned company or a printer purchased from a veteran-owned organization.

Chapter 12

Communications and Marketing

Contributor: Nereida (Neddy) Perez,
Vice President, Inclusion & Diversity, National Grid

Communications is one of the most critical steps in developing, implementing, and managing an effective diversity and inclusion strategy. Without a strong plan in place, executive leaders may not loan their support. If managers and supervisors who are charged with everyday implementation and execution of D&I efforts do not understand what is expected of them, they can disengage. If employees do not know what the long term objectives are, they too can easily get frustrated and feel that D&I is not a priority.

In addition to communicating a company's diversity and inclusion commitment internally, strong correlation exists between the presence of an unyielding diversity commitment and external brand leadership. Leading companies are using communications and marketing efforts to tap the tremendous growth potential that diverse markets represent.

Whether internal or external—through the internet, print media, or word of mouth—the importance of a strong communications and marketing strategy cannot be understated. The purpose of this chapter is to provide a framework that can be customized and used by all companies to create an overall communications and marketing plan to support diversity and inclusion efforts.

In this chapter, we will explore the following questions:

- How should an organization go about developing a communications and marketing plan?

- What people should be engaged in the communications and marketing process?

- How do best practice companies measure the impact of communications and marketing initiatives?

- What types of communications and marketing tools should organizations develop for maximum visibility?

Communications Planning

Most people think that coming up with a communications strategy is complicated, but it is fairly straightforward. Too often a communications plan is overlooked, but it is one of the most crucial areas of D&I strategy. A communications plan should lay out a comprehensive view of how you will communicate each of the core building blocks of your Diversity & Inclusion strategy. There are three building blocks on which you should focus:

- Internal branding should:
  › Promote what the office of D&I is doing
  › Build awareness on what the company and its leadership is committed to
  › Update employees on policy and process changes
  › Increase awareness of the employee network group/employee resource group activities and initiatives
  › Tap into the company newsletter or other media (e.g. podcasts) to communicate D&I efforts
  › Increase connectivity of D&I between leaders and employees

- Learning and Development
  › Promote workshops and learning sessions designed to increase cultural competencies and inclusion skills
  › Increase awareness of events sponsored by employee network groups/employee resource groups that are helping to increase inclusion skills

- External and Media Relations
  › Develop materials to be used at conferences and events focused on inclusion and diversity, recruitment and retention, and customer markets
  › Create and place advertisements outside the company
  › Prepare articles and stories to position the company externally in the media
  › Set up a speakers bureau that helps to develop diverse talent to speak at national and regional conferences or events about the company's D&I efforts
  › Identify nonprofit organizations you want to participate in and negotiate for media presence on their websites and nonprofit publications
  › Identify employees that will serve as spokespeople and can be ready for media interviews related to the company's commitment to Diversity & Inclusion

When developing your communications plan, there are three other areas you will want to consider working very closely with: recruiting, marketing, and supplier diversity. If you are looking to create ads or buy ad space, you will want to make sure the messaging lines up with these three groups, depending on the event or publication in which you will be placing the advertisement. If you are partnering with a professional association that might provide an opportunity to recruit people, you will want to engage recruiting sooner rather than later in the partnership opportunities.

The following is a description of the key components that make up a strong communications plan. You should incorporate these items as you are developing your plan for each focus area mentioned earlier:

- **Define Need/Opportunity** You will want to clearly define what the aims are of your communications plan. Are you looking to address a particular issue? If "yes," then define it in detail. If you are looking to increase overall branding of your D&I strategy, then describe the current state and what you hope to accomplish.

- **Intended Audiences** Describe who it is you want to reach with your messages, including employees, corporate leaders, investors, customers?

- **Goals and Objectives** Clearly define the three to five objectives you want to accomplish with the communications plan.

- **Define How to Implement the Plan** With the help of your communications team you will want to determine what vehicles of communications you will use to implement your plan as well as who should take the lead in implementing certain aspects of the plan. You will need to develop a timeline for implementing the plan.

- **Challenges** Define any potential challenges that you might face. For instance, if you have a small budget, will you need to collaborate or form a partnership with another department/business function in order to secure funding? Are there any people that could potential roadblock your ideas/plans? Is there a potential market condition that can impact your plans? You will also want to think through any potential challenges and come up with some alternatives.

- **Budget** Define what the costs will be to carry out your plan. For instance, will you need to pay for printing costs of a brochure? Will you have to buy promotional items to hand out at an event? Are you planning to bring in a national speaker that you have to pay? Will you be buying ad space in a magazine or establishing an external partnership with a non-profit organization that will require you to make a financial commitment?

- **Measurement and Evaluation** You will want to set some goals on the number of people reached through your various communications vehicles. Also, the communications team will be able to provide guidance on measuring impact of the program whether it is through a straight headcount or survey and assessment plan.

Key People to Engage

There are a number of people you will want to engage in the creation of an D&I communications plan to ensure that materials developed are used/read. Below is a list of the people/departments to connect with and a brief description of why you will want them to be engaged as well as how to engage them:

- **Internal Communications** can develop, design, and write internal materials like announcements of programs and events. The department can also create posters and promotional materials as well as advise you on what the best forms of communications are to reach people.

- **External Communications** can create and edit brochures and press releases and manage media inquiries. They can advise on the best publications to promote the company or the best spokespeople within the company.

- **Community Relations** can help to identify external partnerships that you can collaborate with to strengthen the company's visibility as a strong corporate citizen. They can review articles and provide feedback on ads to make sure the messaging is in sync with the company's diversity mission and external presence.

- **Safety** can review articles and provide feedback on ads to make sure the messaging is in sync with the company's diversity mission and that pictures used are in compliance with safety protocols.

- **Recruiting** can identify external partnerships that you can collaborate on in order to attract diverse talent. They can review articles and provide feedback on ads to make sure that messaging is in sync with the company's diversity mission and their overall attraction goals.

- **Marketing/Consumer Products** can identify external partnerships that you can collaborate on. They can also help develop ideas for articles and review them. Moreover, they can possibly help cover the costs of ad placement or provide guidance on how to get the best advertising prices.

- **Union Relations** can help review articles and advertisements that feature union representatives to ensure that what is said or pictured will not be misconstrued as a violation of a union agreement. Also, the Union Relations Manager/Leader can give you feedback on which people to feature that are role models for the company and/or review articles as well as generate ideas for articles.

- **Legal** can review materials, particularly if external articles are being written on controversial topics that will put the company at risk.

- **Human Resources** can review articles and provide feedback on ads to ensure HR policies and processes are not being violated.

- **Employee Network Group Leaders** can review articles, provide story leads, and serve as resource/subject matter experts to represent the company.

Measuring Impact

There are many ways to track impact. The following are some measures that can be easily tracked in the area of Communications:

- **Advertising Impressions** You can track the total circulation and the cost size of the ad placed. The size of an advertisement will also determine visibility; for instance, a ¾-page ad will not get as much attention as a full page ad.

- **Online Advertising** You can track the number of electronic impressions received on your particular page.

- **Non-Paid Articles** These are articles that are not purchased and/or written as advertorials. These can be tracked based on size of the article written as well as the placement of the article. A front page story, for instance, will yield a bigger readership rate than a third page article. In magazines, a double page spread and length of article will also matter.

- **Paid Articles/Advertorials** These can be assessed based on the size of the advertisement and the readership.

- **Speaking Engagements** You can track the number of external public speaking engagements by accounting for the total number of attendees in the session.

- **Conference Presence** You can track total number of conferences and total (actual) number of attendees at the conference/event being sponsored.

- **Non-Profit Board Positions** If you have secured any positions, you will want to track the number of board positions and the organization's membership.

Developing Communications Materials

The following is a list of the critical communications materials that you will want, at bare minimum, to help raise awareness about your company's D&I efforts:

- **Advertisement** Contract an agency or your in-house communications team to create a series of advertisements designed to promote your company's diversity efforts. Following is a short list of ads:

  › A generic diversity ad that can be easily modified in various sizes that can be reproduced

  › An advertisement for use at conferences

› An advertisement for use by your Recruiting department. Work with recruiting to make sure they are not creating their own advertisement. The ad should depict a wide range of individuals.

- **Annual Report** If your D&I department and initiatives are new, you may want to wait two to three years before you create an annual report to give you time development and accumulate information about your programs. If you feel you have enough information and your programs are well-established, definitely create a comprehensive report to help highlight your D&I efforts and achievements.

- **Brochure to Promote Diversity & Inclusion Function** Create a general brochure designed to promote the work of the Office of Diversity & Inclusion.

- **Brochure to Promote Employee Network Groups** In order for employee network groups to grow and be understood, they need to be promoted.

- **Brochure for Diversity Recruiting** This brochure should be developed in conjunction with your recruiting team and should include a letter from the president and head of diversity about the important of inclusion and diversity. Employees in a wide range of positions should be depicted.

- **Employee Network Group/Resource Group Handbook** If you have employee network groups/employee resource groups (ERGs), develop a set of guidelines for operation.

- **Message from the President** This is a critical piece to create for use on your company website, in your company brochure, and in your new employee orientation folder.

- **Website** Your website should have section dedicated to diversity and inclusion. Develop the site in conjunction with the company's Communications Team. The site should include at a minimum:

  › A President's message

  › A message from the head of D&I

  › Tabs or sections for the employee network groups

  › A list of diversity resources (books for reading; videos available to be used, leaders in the company, etc.)

  › A list of training opportunities available within the company

  › Links to other company functions, such as Recruiting, Human Resources, etc.

Conclusion

In this chapter, we:

- Recommended key steps in developing a communications and marketing plan.

- Discussed who should be engaged in the communications and marketing process.

- Shared how best practices companies measure the impact of communications and marketing initiatives.

- Summarized the types of communications and marketing tools organizations should develop for maximum visibility.

Best practice companies understand that their growth and livelihood are highly dependent on an overarching and sustainable diversity and inclusion plan that is communicated effectively. Through a wealth of new and innovative resources, such as social media and networking, and through tried and true techniques, such as print media and word of mouth marketing, these companies are building committed employees and loyal consumers.

Maintaining and growing a diversity and inclusion commitment, from workplace to market-place, suppliers to consumers, requires extensive communication internally and externally, and across all functions and geographies. However, arriving at a strong and trusted diversity and inclusion brand—brought to life through meaningful action—is no quick and easy task. This takes time, dedication, resources, and above all, a true belief that diversity and inclusion is a vital corporate asset.

Case Study:
Walt Disney Parks & Resorts

No strategy can be successful without a communication plan, one that informs employees, shareholders, and consumers alike. Strategic communication ensures that everyone is on the same page about values, best practices, and policies, especially when it comes to implementing diversity and encouraging inclusion. In doing so, many companies and organizations choose to use a top-down approach, but that is only effective when the "down" is aware of and informed about what the "top" is doing.

Walt Disney Parks & Resorts is a massive organization, one that encompasses multiple international theme parks that cover hundreds of square miles, require tens of thousands of employees, and draw hundreds of thousands of guests. Communicating to all of these audiences is nearly impossible. Walt Disney Parks & Resorts recognizes this, and instead of addressing the general populations, it targets its communications to niche groups with special needs. One such group is people with disabilities.

Walt Disney Parks & Resorts, like most successful companies, begins its diversity communication with the employees. "We inform our cast of our vision, mission, and action plan though inclusion of diversity presentations in our monthly information sessions, our quarterly updates, and our written communication media on e-mail," says the company of its diversity recruitment strategy. The global locations and seemingly universal appeal of Disney naturally draw a multicultural consumer base. The vast, diverse nature of the guests and the physical nature of the attractions combine to present a unique problem: many guests with disabilities want to visit and enjoy a Walt Disney park or resort, but cannot because of physical or mental conditions.

Guest Assistance Cards (GACs) were the first step taken by Walt Disney Parks & Resorts to address this problem. This card allows for extended access and privileges to guests that need assistance or special care. A GAC is a very personalized, one-on-one form of communication between individual guests and "cast members," or Disney employees. The card tells cast members what a guest's needs are and can make for a much easier experience.

In addition to GACs, a publication entitled Walt Disney World® with Disabilities, an unofficial resource that was written from the experiences of people with health conditions, has been instrumental in communicating Disney's commitment to serving people with disabilities. The book provides useful information about hotels, parks, shops, restaurants, and rides and is aimed at people with minor to major health issues, special needs, and disabilities. It discusses, for example, what rides are intense or fear-based that could cause trauma for children or those with phobias. It also ranks the rides based on comfort, speed, and level of physical strain. Moreover, Walt Disney World® with Disabilities offers support for diet issues as well as tips for transportation and wheelchair use.

In addition to the book, there is an exhaustive supplemental website which provides free content and information about the physical and emotional "feel" of Disney World rides and attractions. It also educates guests about the wide variety of guest support services the resorts offer of which most guests are not aware. This allows for a more enjoyable experience for all involved when traveling to a Walt Disney park or resort.

Case Study:
Merrill Lynch & Co., Inc.

Merrill Lynch begins external outreach through internal support for diversity. Employee networks and affinity groups provide the research and basis for marketing and advertising techniques to various minority groups. The drive behind new diversity marketing strategies comes from within. This allows for Merrill Lynch to have one of the most inclusive marketing and advertising plans not only among investment bankers and wealth managers, but also among all U.S.-based global companies.

The Multicultural Marketing group creates integrated marketing programs for multicultural investors and business with a high net worth to help establish Merrill Lynch as the financial services leader. The main focus of this is to increase brand relevance in diverse communities and to expand development into new business markets. Part of the company's marketing strategy are its strategic alliances with Merrill Lynch's affinity groups and targeted messaging that takes into account all cultural and societal factors. For example, the company forms community-based partnerships with African-American organizations. It aims to capture their growing market share through programming that resonates with wealthy African Americans. The company also aims to establish a market share for affluent Hispanics through these same strategies.

The Merrill Lynch Native American Banking and Financial Services initiative seeks to establish relationships with Native American tribal governments, enterprises, and members. It currently serves more than 60 tribes, and the company has a long history as an advisor to several tribal governments.

Merrill Lynch's South Asian Marketing Efforts initiative focuses on identifying and meeting the financial needs of individuals from India, Pakistan, Nepal, Bangladesh, and Sri Lanka by creating awareness. In addition, Merrill Lynch provides educational materials and seminars targeted to the financial needs of affluent South Asians.

The LGBT program focuses on organizations at local and national levels, instead of being community-based. Merrill Lynch wants to establish brand relevance in the LGBT market and is developing specialized services for domestic partners. Special Needs Marketing focuses on affluent families who have children/adults with special needs by providing specialized wealth management tools, trained Financial Advisors, and customized solutions that address the particular financial needs of each family situation.

The Women's Marketing program, led by 28 Managing Directors, works to increase brand relevance while empowering and attracting female investors to Merrill Lynch. It encourages women to work together to address unique business needs and is primarily focused on boomer women and women in transition. It also holds an annual investor conference for women clients to bring them together with Merrill Lynch's product and market specialists.

Chapter 13

Community Relations and Philanthropy

Increasingly, organizations seeking to be global industry leaders are realizing that employees and consumers alike are closely scrutinizing not only a company's goods and services, but its community efforts as well. Strong community relations and corporate philanthropy efforts should be a key component of any company's overall business strategy, and these efforts should continually adapt to the changing needs of the communities in which employees and customers live and work.

Does the company show a genuine care for the people it serves and not just the bottom line? How is foundation money allocated, and to which groups? Do employees volunteer? Does this commitment cross local and national borders? The answers to these questions can ultimately determine whether a potential customer decides to buy a company's product or whether a potential employee decides to apply for a position with the organization.

In this chapter, we will explore the following questions:

- What are the current trends in community relations and philanthropy, particularly as they relate to diversity and inclusion?

- What are the strategic steps of effective community relations and philanthropy programs?

- Who are the key players and audiences of a successful community relations and philanthropy plans?

- What is the role of employee network and affinity groups in community relations and philanthropy?

- How should an organization measure the impact and success of community relations and philanthropy initiatives?

Community Relations Trends

These days, Corporate Social Responsibility (CSR) has moved beyond compliance to become instead a central factor in determining corporate success and authenticity. As such, CSR is increasingly about how a company earns profits, as opposed to focusing on how profits are spent. Some other important CSR trends include:

- **Strategic alignment** Corporations are re-aligning community relations, philanthropy, foundations and other progressive functions to be more strategic.

- **Diversified giving portfolio** The portfolio of corporate giving, in addition to cash and in-kind donations, now includes cause-related marketing, community partnerships, workplace giving campaigns, employee volunteer programs and fundraising. Company contributions have become more results oriented, reflecting a corporation's business goals.

- **Focusing on fewer causes** Companies are directing their contributions to fewer causes, thus avoiding stakeholder confusion and dilution of the corporate social mission.

- **Greater need for business support** The need for business leaders to play an active role in civic affairs is increasing, especially since the government has reduced its involvement and delegated much of its responsibility to the local level.

- **Cause selection aligned with corporate strategy** Best-practice companies leverage their unique capabilities in support of social causes that fit their corporate positioning and strategy.

- **Evaluation of ROI** Companies are tracking returns on investments such as improved morale, stock price and stakeholder relations.

- **Greater accountability** Companies are challenged to determine what to be accountable for, who they should be accountable to, and how they will demonstrate this responsibility. Information is now easy to gather through corporate websites.

- **Transparent reporting** Meaningful corporate social responsibility reporting today requires that companies share both successes and failures with stakeholders. Honest, candid, transparent disclosures often garner greater trust and loyalty.

- **Expanded definition of "community"** Although "community" has traditionally meant the community directly surrounding the company's operations, today it includes an array of communities, such as those where employees live and work, where customers are located, where supplier operations reside, and where raw materials are acquired.

- **Expanded reporting mediums** The increased flow of communications, especially from media sources, has cast attention on corporate behavior. This has prompted an increase in reporting of corporate-responsibility, environmental-impact, and sustainability reports.

- **More value given to community partnerships** Companies and non-profits are increasingly creating more integrated partnerships (previously limited to corporate sponsorship and philanthropic donations) that advance the missions of both partners as well as the company's bottom line. Cause-related marketing and workforce development are common practices.

- **Diversity and Inclusion** Diversity and inclusion as a component of CSR is gaining momentum and attention. Diversity is now linked to business objectives throughout best-practices companies.

Strategic Contributions Plan

A plan for community involvement and giving should be a joint effort forged amongst community relations, corporate communications, foundation executives, and the corporate diversity and inclusion officer. Some key factors to consider when crafting a contributions plan include:

- **Alignment** Alignment between corporate giving and corporate mission has never been more significant, and the synergies with community relations, corporate communications, and marketing functions have never been stronger. In best-practices companies, we witness an alignment of functions and the ability to have greater synergy. Today's companies are approaching community relations in a more strategic way. They set goals and objectives. Companies try to figure out what it means to be a good corporate citizen, how they can involve the workforce and leadership, and achieve a return on investment.

- **Volunteer opportunities** Many employees are interested in volunteer work, and smart companies are finding ways to channel that impulse into activities that help the business. For example, Fannie Mae and Freddie Mac provide support for low-income community activities, while AARP gives a day off for community relations projects, such as Habitat for Humanity.

- **Partnership** Partnerships with universities and organizations have never been stronger, with support tied to a corporation's foundation or philanthropic efforts.

- **Input** This can involve requests from affinity groups. It also may come from employees (and matching grants), from stakeholders, or perhaps from those diversity third parties that have a clear plan of alignment for a company. It can come directly from the diversity team and the diversity council(s).

- **Coordination** Because of the growing number of philanthropic efforts on the part of corporations, unprecedented coordination and communication is required. All companies are linking their efforts to diversity and women's activities as never before. The relationships require functional integration to support philanthropic interests.

- **Plans and Goals** Within the overall community relations strategy, companies must ensure all diversity questions are considered, including objectives, numbers of people to be reached and other such areas.

- **Personnel** Best-practice companies are employing a dedicated person responsible for coordinating with their PR staff. The community relations director generally reports to the top corporate communications officer; however, a dotted reporting line connects to others in the diversity office. The community relations and diversity offices must work together to create an effective program.

- **Measurement** Community relations must be measured closely and the results weighed, especially since areas of giving are often changed to meet the interests of the company, its customer base and its employees' interests and involvements.

Audiences: Local & Global

It is imperative that all audiences hear, understand, and embrace a company's community relations and social responsibility platforms. The global impact of companies has never been more apparent. As such, social responsibility should be sensitive to both local and global implications. Research should document the impact of initiatives on local, national, and global communities to demonstrate how corporate values can bridge any cultural and economic divides.

Local Community

The most progressive companies try to make a positive impact on communities far before they even engage in business operations. For example, Home Depot is committed to meeting with civic and community leaders to discuss how they might provide resources or lead initiatives in a community before opening a store, and they communicate the accomplishments of each meeting on their website.

National Community

On the national level, large companies seek to cultivate an image of social responsibility, community mindedness, and financial generosity. Johnson & Johnson, for one, with 200 companies operating in 54 countries, is committed to improving the quality of life around the world. To that end, the company and its affiliates sponsor programs and team with local charities and social organizations to give back to the communities where they do business.

Global Community

In the global economy, it is becoming more and more important for companies to respect and contribute to the world as a whole. Leading in importance are issues relating to world health, population and the environment. Leading, community-minded companies stay abreast of issues of importance to world audiences. With this knowledge, they construct their global community relations strategy. Their challenge is to balance the national identity and the initiatives that stem from it with those of the global communities with which it does business.

When expanding into new countries, a proactive social strategy is key to winning the good faith of the community, government, and stakeholders with which relations must be formed. For example, global furniture-maker Herman Miller has organized nine environmental groups that work in a number of areas to oversee its environmental philosophy. One of these groups has made considerable efforts to send production materials to the compost pile as opposed to the landfill. Another group has been working to save energy for the company that has resulted in approximately $1 million in savings.

Employee Networks

Employee networks are experiencing an increase in importance at progressive companies. These networks are a valuable source of information about feelings and attitudes of certain community groups. This information may be especially useful in determining minority needs in the community.

General Mills, for example, uses its diversity networks to reach out to the community. Its Asia-Pacific group helps with a program for the Chinese New Year that is sponsored by General Mills throughout local schools. General Mills also sponsors the Martin Luther King Parade and a Black Family Reunion, both of which serve to bring community members together to celebrate multiculturalism, and its Latin American group helps to sponsor the Telemundo Essay Contest that asks students to describe how being a Latin American encompasses the best of both worlds. All of these programs are used to help the employees and community members maintain pride in their heritage.

Measurement

Effective measurement tools are needed to prove how corporate community relations improve the bottom line. To quantify the strategic impact of community relations, leading companies are accounting for every dollar spent while articulating the benefits to all involved. Best-practice companies use research and measurement to evaluate their programs both before and after implementation.

One way to measure community relations programs is by their outcome:

- Do they link with educational programs that can aid recruiting, including internship partners?

- Do they access to women and minority talent?

- Do they create new entry points for products or services?

- Do they support community-based organizations or causes that are important to the company or a group of employees?

- Do they connect the company with minority and women suppliers?

- Do they provide external recognition?

- Do they provide media coverage?

Corporate Philanthropy

Today, the diversity and inclusion officer and team are playing a greater role in philanthropy. Today, philanthropy is not motivated by altruism alone, but by enlightened corporate and employee interests. Today's leading companies choose to utilize their resources with increased care, evaluation, and attention. Philanthropic contributions and community relations are implicitly understood to be both a cost of doing business and a requisite to success.

Key steps in creating an effective philanthropic giving program include:

- **Integrate philanthropy into strategic goals and company mission.** Rather than regarding philanthropy as separate from business operations, companies align both their strategic and business goals. They make sure the strategy pivots around employee, customer, community, and other stakeholders' areas of interest.

- **Connect philanthropy with other community programs.** Connecting charitable donations with other community involvement activities maximizes the impact of a company's giving campaign. New trends show that "social investment" can increase impact, at a lower cost, by providing a mix of benefits of greater value to partners through more efficient means for the company.

- **Budget appropriately.** Although there are a variety of budgeting methods, companies must be sure to allocate their funds appropriately and update the budget as necessary. Some budgeting methods include: predetermined percentage, sliding percentage based on profitability, fixed percentage, per-capita, and fixed dollar.

- **Ensure effective program infrastructure.** Companies must determine the infrastructure that will provide the desired legal and tax outcomes. Nonprofit corporate foundations and direct donations are two examples.

- **Formalize policies and guidelines for funding.** When establishing guidelines, ensure consistency with the organization's values and objectives. Policies should outline: focus areas, issues of interest, and types of programs/organizations it will support. Many institutions also create written policies describing their decision-making processes and grant criteria. Websites are a great communication source for these objectives.

- **Involve employees in philanthropic activities.** Employee involvement is critical for the success of philanthropic objectives. Employees should play an active role in determining which causes to support and who will be awarded grants. Matched giving and employee volunteerism are also wonderful initiatives that initiate success.

- **Incorporate stakeholder communication.** Companies may incorporate a range of stakeholders into their programs and solicit feedback. Companies also accept external stakeholders to donate to their causes, sometimes including incentives.

- **Develop long-term business/nonprofit partnerships.** Developing long-term relationships with the organizations they support creates group/issue affiliation and aids nonprofit organizations due to creation of guaranteed support levels.

Process of Diversity and Inclusion Philanthropy

Input

Requests may come from affinity groups. They may come from employees, stakeholders, or third parties that have a clear plan for aligning with the company's mission. They can come directly from the diversity team or the diversity council(s).

Coordination

Companies must coordinate and communicate if they want to link their philanthropy efforts to diversity and women's issues. These relationships require functional integration and connecting the dots between different areas of the corporation.

Plan and Goals

Smart companies make a plan for their overall giving, including diversity interests. This plan should include objectives, numbers of people to be reached, and other such areas.

Communications

Smart companies with strong diversity programs communicate internally and externally. Increasingly, companies are publishing information on their philanthropy programs in various formats:

- In the annual report

- In a special diversity annual report or quarterly report

- In special reports to stockholders and employees

- On the Internet

- On their Intranet

Measurement and Evaluation

To maintain a successful, enduring philanthropy program, companies should thoroughly evaluate the impact of their donations and the value and effectiveness of their programs and individual grants regularly. Countless measurement mechanisms exist with which to do so.

Furthermore, it is critical that nonprofit organizations understand that they are accountable for the use of their funds. Therefore, it is in their best interest, as well as the interest of the donor, to assess the results of their philanthropic program.

While many organizations recognize the importance of philanthropic activities, they are under increasing pressure to demonstrate both value and return on investment. Effective measurement of initiatives provides countless benefits. Not only does it quantify the impact of philanthropic endeavors, but it also enables them to make a case for at-risk activities and promote successes throughout the corporate channels.

Measurement Mechanisms

There is no best way by which companies can measure the success of their contribution programs. Companies now measure philanthropy to weigh results. A good program will shift resources to meet the needs of the company, its customer base, and its employees.

Evaluation and Reporting

The extent of evaluation procedures typically varies depending on the size of each individual grant. For smaller grants, a brief report at the end of the year explaining how the funds were used is usually adequate. For larger contributions, however, the report should be more detailed. Project objectives, expected financial impacts, key accomplishments, recipients, time schedules, anticipated results, and other relevant information should be thoughtfully integrated into a thorough and inclusive report. These tools allow stakeholders to conclude whether the planned objectives and anticipated goals are being met effectively and with little to no wasted resources.

Conclusion

In this chapter, we:

- Revealed current trends in community relations and philanthropy, particularly as they relates to diversity and inclusion.

- Explored strategic steps to effective community relations and philanthropy programs.

- Determined the key players and audiences of successful community relations and philanthropy initiatives.

- Analyzed the role of employee network and affinity groups in community relations and philanthropy.

- Shared how organizations can measure the impact and success of community relations and philanthropy initiatives.

The success of any organization is based on reciprocal relationships between any number of vital players—such as employees, customers, stakeholders, lawmakers, and suppliers, among many others. Creating and nurturing these relationships is just as important to a company's success as the quality of its products and services. Through efforts such as educational programs, volunteerism, environmental protection initiatives, and fundraising events, companies are able to strengthen their brand while establishing a close connection with those they serve.

Community relations and corporate philanthropy can be an effective tool for companies that are trying to meet employees' and consumers' rising expectations of the role businesses should play in society. It is not enough to say the right things; companies that wish to remain competitive in years to come must embrace social responsibility through words and actions. Ultimately, the goodwill of the company will yield positive results in the community which will in turn boost sales. Bottom line? It's a win-win scenario for all involved.

Case Study: KPMG International

The values of KPMG, a global network of firms providing audit and tax services, directly shape and define the company's culture and identity. So when it says, "We are committed to our communities," it means something. It means 12,000 employees and partners volunteer each year in their regions. It means 500,000 hours are donated to Corporate Social Responsibility (CSR) every year by member firms. It means 700 local volunteer events take place annually around the world. These practices not only expose KPMG employees to more diversity externally, but also bring diversity into the workplace.

KPMG in Shanghai supports Operation Smile, helping to provide 125 operations for children with cleft lips and palettes in China. KPMG in Brazil runs a program that allows 220 poor children to receive computer lessons, medical treatment, and sports activities. KPMG in Sri Lanka and Thailand worked hard to raise money after a devastating tsunami to build five villages with homes for over 180 families. Internationally, KPMG firms from Ecuador to Germany to South Africa donated 3.5 million dollars in aid to the communities affected by the recent tsunami.

With a presence in 148 countries, it is essential that KPMG continually strengthens its image and reputation around the world. As a responsible corporate citizen, it does just that. It betters international and diverse areas through employees' hard work and a commitment to communities. In turn, this creates a more inclusive global economy, one that is supported by the United National Global Compact. The Compact's principles correlate closely with KPMG's values. There are also tangible business benefits to being socially responsible. A philanthropic attitude attracts more clients, particularly diverse clients, while opening up new consumer markets.

Internally, the benefits are numerous as well. KPMG attracts a more diverse employee population with its breakthrough corporate philanthropy. These new employees bring with them the skill set that KPMG wants for the entire company, a skill set where awareness and acceptance of cultures is critical for success. However, KPMG's Corporate Social Responsibility also promotes diverse thinking for current employees as well. It develops these crucial diversity skills through action and contact with other populations. Overall, it makes employees more dynamic and open-minded.

Corporate responsibility and diversity are very closely linked at KPMG, believes with Lord Michael Hastings, global head of citizenship and diversity. "This responsible approach helps us maintain our leadership position as a recognized brand, highly respected for our people," says Hastings. "You can't understate the extra sense of purpose and self-worth that people develop when they feel they are genuinely making a difference and helping to create a better world for everyone."

Case Study: Walmart

At Walmart, diversity and inclusion is not something that is simply talked about; it is engrained in the company's identity. From community support and corporate giving, to associate programs and recruitment efforts, diversity and inclusion is interwoven in everything Walmart does.

Through Walmart's Diversity Relations Department, the company has developed and maintained valuable relationships with diverse organizations and key influencers. Walmart is proud to partner with more than 400 diverse community organizations nationwide and selects each of these diverse community partnerships by truly looking at the areas that affect them at the local and national level. By focusing on educational initiatives, economic empowerment, leadership development, financial independence, and health and wellness, these relationships position the company to better support the issues that are important to its associates, partners, and communities.

To illustrate one area of involvement, Walmart has actively been involved with the Thurgood Marshall Scholarship Fund. In 2007, Walmart donated $1 million to the organization for the creation of the "Strive for Excellence" Scholarship to benefit students attending public Historically Black Colleges and Universities. The money helps first-generation African-American college students get an education.

At Walmart, the company does its best to connect its relationships with community organizations to its business goals as a company. Sam's Club partners with the Women Presidents' Organization (WPO) to produce an event focused on educating children on the key financial principles of savings, finance, and money management. The event, CASHFLOW for Kids, develops young people's financial intelligence through a board game. With financial independence and education as two of Walmart's major focuses, this partnership really allows the company to connect with this particular community while maintaining its business goals.

As a good neighbor, Walmart strengthens the communities it serves by creating new jobs, collecting billions in state and local taxes, participating on governing boards of community organizations, protecting acres of wildlife habitat, and providing charitable contributions.

Walmart believes in a philosophy of operating globally and giving back locally. Through the Walmart and Sam's Club Foundation, associates have the option of giving to charitable organizations through payroll deductions. Some of these organizations include the United Negro College Fund, Hispanic Scholarship Fund, and the Asian and Pacific Islander American Scholarship Fund. The company also matches donations to these organizations dollar for dollar up to $1 million.

Additionally, in 2005 Walmart established Associate Resource Groups to promote diversity and inclusion and create a sense of community among associates sharing similar backgrounds and interests. These groups are committed to advancing the company's bottom line by leveraging the diversity of associates to become an employer and retailer of choice in the communities served.

While Walmart looks forward to growing to serve more and more communities, the company will also continue to strive for the best possible partnerships to help as many communities save money as possible so they can live better. As Walmart reflects on its accomplishments and celebrates its successes, the company looks forward to continuing the progress it has made and fully integrating diversity into all business units.

Chapter 14

Global Diversity and Inclusion

Today, an ever-changing global marketplace and labor force demands continue to challenge long-held business assumptions and force major structural reorganizations at many companies across key business, marketing, and talent recruitment and retention functions. The global gold rush for multicultural markets, diverse employees, and untapped consumer bases has already begun. Globalization is a powerful buzzword in corporate circles, and corporate leaders are eager to establish a strong presence in a variety of emerging markets. New commercial innovations and powerful technologies are truly bringing the world's best products and services right to our doorsteps.

Global diversity, like domestic diversity, offers rich opportunities for company growth through an increased talent pool, wider consumer base, and additional revenue streams. Yet, global diversity and inclusion initiatives face particularly challenging aspects, such as geographical distance, different time zones, virtual relationships, language barriers, and distinctive cultural values, actions, and assumptions.

Success in global markets will require more than boutique multicultural initiatives. Competing on a multinational playing field will require a sustained effort to integrate distinct cultural and more inclusive values into a newer and broader vision for company growth and advancement.

In this chapter, we will explore the following questions:

• How do best practice companies create a sustainable global diversity and inclusion structure?

• What must an organization do to achieve corporate understanding of global diversity and inclusion best practices?

• Who are the key players in a global diversity and inclusion team?

• How should the success of global diversity and inclusion initiatives be measured? What accountability systems should be established toward this end?

Creating Sustainable Global Diversity and Inclusion

In the twenty-first century, rapid globalization requires a new look at diversity. Imposing U.S.-based diversity and inclusion initiatives onto an international playing field without thoughtful regard to the distinctions that create business identities and cultures can result in tense relationships and misunderstanding, as well as loss in revenue, staff, and credibility.

While diversity in the United States may speak to equality and inclusion along the lines of gender, race, disability, age, religion, and sexual orientation, this definition may not apply directly to a nation where hierarchical race or gender ranks are the norm. This is not to suggest that U.S. companies should dispose of their current values surrounding diversity and inclusion, but rather that companies should be open to adapting to and learning from other cultures, thus creating a universal definition that speaks to a global audience and can be tailored to local regions.

To effectively address global D&I issues, organizations must understand how having diversity in workforce representation, as well as in the way the company thinks and approaches strategic issues, will bring greater value to the company and its stakeholders.

In developing global diversity programs, most corporate strategic planning processes focus on the four "As": Analysis, Action planning, Alignment, and Assessment.

- **Analysis:** Begin by analyzing your existing internal structures and capabilities as they relate to the demands and opportunities of the external global business environment. Ask where are we now, and where do want to go?

- **Action planning:** Create strategic goals based on the gap analysis and by utilizing the diversity strengths and ideas of your global team, develop specific action plans to reach these goals. Ask now that we know where we want to go, how do we get there?

- **Alignment:** Align the strategic action plan with the existing infrastructure of your company, infusing global D&I initiatives across all levels and divisions for maximum sustainability. Ask how do we make our global D&I initiatives an everyday part of our existence, rather than a passing trend?

- **Assessment:** Assess implementation results through measurement and accountability tools. These tools should measure progress on the global D&I goals set during the "action planning" stage. Ask are we progressing toward our goals, and, if not, what do we need to change?

Devoting adequate corporate time and resources to these four pertinent steps is fundamental in building a global program that is truly embedded into the company fabric. All too often,

D&I programs are spearheaded under one individual's leadership only to fade in that person's absence. Given the corporate investment it takes to develop a D&I program and the amount of return that can be achieved through these initiatives, companies cannot afford to reinvent the wheel every time a corporate leadership change occurs.

The goal is to create corporate cultural change through institutional changes that is lasting over time. This can only be done through development of a formal global D&I initiative that is reflected in corporate values, programs, and day-to-day conduct. Best-practice organizations integrate global diversity into day-to-day operations to ensure that it is ongoing and contributes to corporate D&I and business results.

In creating a global D&I structure, companies should:

- Build a global team that reflects the company's diverse global employee, consumer, and shareholder base

- Create a shared understanding of what the company means by "global diversity and inclusion"

- Give responsibility and ownership to line employees and local organizations, while providing centralized monitoring and support

- Engage senior leaders and hold them accountable

- Establish network and affinity groups and diversity councils (in a manner compatible with a company's culture and employee relations philosophy)

- Provide training to the entire workforce with particular focus on management and executive training

- Incorporate D&I into mentoring efforts and leadership training

- Foster communication channels for sharing and learning throughout the organization

- Develop assessment tools for measuring progress on an ongoing basis.

The following sections will explore three of these areas in greater depth: creating a shared corporate understanding of global D&I, building a global team, and developing assessment tools for measuring progress.

Achieving Corporate Understanding of Global D&I

Global D&I does not yet have a universally shared definition. The myriad of definitions that do exist stem from each definer's subjective framework and are influenced by national context, political agenda, dominant culture, religion, and gender, among other factors, creating an ongoing fluctuation of the term "global diversity and inclusion."

A company's global mission statement should not and cannot be mere rhetoric if the company plans on succeeding in its endeavors. Far too many companies lack a true understanding and commitment to global diversity. Without a clear and shared vision of global D&I throughout the organization, global efforts will only prove to shift the company laterally rather than propel it forward.

The organization's global vision must go beyond the standard one for domestic diversity and acknowledge the global reach and cultural differences inherent in doing business both in and among different countries. The end goal is to become increasingly more competitive and innovative throughout the world by fostering common areas within diversity and inclusion, globally and locally.

Further, companies must reflect by asking, "Are we honestly being inclusive of other cultures and ideas in creating our definition of global diversity and inclusion, or are we merely trying to impose our U.S.-centric views on others?" It is naïve to believe that in a world as large and diverse as ours, one country or one people holds supreme knowledge. Nonetheless, these notions exist in many companies that do business worldwide and must be set aside before corporate cohesion and key partnerships can form to build global initiatives.

A few questions corporations should ask as they create a common definition of global D&I are:

- How do American value statements underlying domestic diversity and inclusion efforts need to be altered to have meaning and relevance outside the United States?

- What are our basic beliefs and assumptions underlying diversity?

- Where do they converge with other nations?

- How can we tailor our definition to local regions for greater acceptance and effectiveness?

Three guiding principles for global D&I:

- **Respect core human values.** Human dignity and basic rights should remain paramount regardless of the country/region in which you are doing business.

- **Respect local traditions.** You cannot expect to change the traditions and culture of the country/region in which you are doing business.

- **Find common ground.** Understand that there will be possible areas of disagreement when intersecting universal ideas with local context, yet strive to find the common areas and use them as a starting point for moving your global.

Building a Global Diversity and Inclusion Team

Global diversity and inclusion teams, like corporate global D&I mission statements, should reflect their function by being internationally representative and inclusive. While this may seem like common sense, oftentimes corporations pull together "global" teams that appear haphazard rather than strategic, domestic rather than global.

Bringing diverse groups of people to work together is not enough. True diversity encompasses inclusion and not just sheer representation. In order for companies to be successful in their global approach, they must not only bring together key global players, but also create a space for all members to contribute in a meaningful way.

To achieve this, corporations can leverage their worldwide human capital by choosing team members from different nations and regions, corporate levels, genders, sexual orientations, generations, ability groups, and skill sets. Differences create barriers when not managed well, yet when viewed and utilized as assets they can help to achieve results that are more innovative and comprehensive than those stemming from homogeneous groups.

Globally-diverse teams can benefit by paying special attention to the following best practices:

- **Team Function** Clarify roles and functions. The job of the team is to design, implement, assess, and explain the company's global diversity initiative. The team should be able to identify key diversity issues globally, locally, regionally, and by country and tie them directly to the company's business objectives.

- **Work Process** Formulate a shared team process. Initially, it is important for the team to discuss and clarify expectations about how members will work together, including approaches to meeting protocol, decision making, and feedback.

- **Cultural Diversity** Create an environment that encourages the team to draw upon the diverse cultural backgrounds of its members. Awareness of the diverse styles each team member brings to the team process is the first step; leveraging diversity for improved team results requires steady attention and commitment from all team members.

- **Conflict Resolution** Utilize inquiry and open-ended questions with the goal of understanding team members' perspectives. The process of discovering the reasons behind differing perspectives frequently leads to a new openness on all sides and to solutions that could not have been reached in the absence of this information.

- **Information Exchange** Build communication systems for flowing information easily and frequently between members. While most global teams meet virtually, invest in at least one face-to-face team meeting at the beginning of the team's interactions to establish rapport.

Although the challenge of leading global teams remains a concern for many, the business case for increasing the number of worldwide diversity teams is solid and will only continue to expand in line with the global market. If structured and supported adequately through corporate resources and strong backing from leadership, global teams can excel in terms of efficiency, innovation, and outcomes.

Establishing Accountability and Measurement Systems

To be effective, organizations must tie all diversity and inclusion initiatives directly to measurable outcomes. However, assessing the impact of a global D&I initiative can be challenging given the different reporting requirements and laws from country to country, especially as they pertain to representation numbers. Nonetheless, the critical step is to move forward in customizing a measurement system that speaks to the company's goals to ensure reflection, feedback, and accountability.

Successful global leaders measure success in global diversity and inclusion as they measure other business factors. Some examples of metrics include:

- Diversity representation (particularly in senior level positions)

- Hires, promotions, turnover by gender, nationality, ethnicity, etc.

- Achievement of strategic global diversity goals

- Sales in diverse, global markets

- Employee survey scores

- Conference and event survey feedback

- Customer satisfaction by demographic segment

- Number of complaints or legal actions

Benchmarking is another powerful tool in gauging the gap between a company's present global diversity status and the level it needs to reach to be among best practice organizations. Some benchmarking strategies include:

Identify areas for improvement. Since benchmarking can be applied to a wide range of business areas, a variety of research techniques should be utilized. These tools include: surveys, quantitative data collection and research, focus groups, marketing research, and qualitative information gathering through methods such as informal meetings and observations.

Identify organizations that are leaders in these areas. Confer with industry contacts, search the internet, consult trade associations, and survey customers to determine the companies that are paragons in your areas of global diversity focus.

Research best-practice organizations. Best-practice companies share a wealth of knowledge about their global practices and procedures on their websites, in interviews and articles, and at conferences and seminars. Conduct research on these best practices or hire a consult to research on your behalf and tailor the findings to fit your company's business goals.

Infuse best practice strategies into corporate infrastructure. Harness these leading edge practices by developing implementation plans which include funding the initiatives, selling the business case, and garnering organizational leadership support.

Measurement as it relates to accountability is a continuous process in which organizations constantly seek to challenge their practices. Indeed, setting new goals and challenges will be a continuing exercise for global organizations.

Conclusion

In this chapter, we:

- Studied how best practices companies create a sustainable global diversity and inclusion structure.

- Assessed how to achieve corporate understanding of global D&I best practices.

- Considered who the key players are in a global diversity and inclusion team.

- Discussed effective ways to measuring and establishing accountability for the success of global diversity and inclusion initiatives.

Ready or not, globalization is rapidly changing the landscape of the business world, and global diversity and inclusion requires a new corporate playbook to create sustainable, long-term success. Without this approach, leaders risk entering a country's borders only to realize as they delve deeper, that larger issues are at stake, forcing them to retreat when they do not have quick answers. If corporations are myopic and only view global D&I as strictly a manufacturing or operational issue, they risk failure of the business objective but also of future reputation in foreign markets.

The most insightful leaders know that even within the United States, adapting to the specific region and culture is a key factor in whether or not business flourishes. To remain competitive, corporate executives must make a conscious and distinct shift in vision around definitions of diversity and inclusion in a global marketplace, and they must embrace global D&I as not only a necessity, but as a true asset to increase sustainability, profit, and shareholder value.

Case Study: AT&T Inc.

The United States offers a wide consumer base and a rich employee talent pool. AT&T knows this—it's the nation's largest wireless carrier based on subscribers. But beyond U.S. borders, AT&T has effectively tapped the international market as well. It is the world's largest telecommunications company with $120 billion in revenues and more than 100 million international customers. It carries more than 13.4 petabytes of data traffic daily to nearly every continent and country. It conducts business in more than 150 languages and provides specific services and products for the diverse customer base.

Naturally, the 309,050 AT&T employees worldwide are as diverse as the company's customers. AT&T values individual perspectives and promotes an environment of inclusion. Women make up 44 percent of all employees. People of color make up 35 percent of U.S. employees. There are more than 1,700 AT&T reps working in 22 Call Centers that provide service and information to 1.5 million customers in languages other than English.

Clearly, the removal of barriers in employment allows for recruitment from a wider global talent pool, longer retention of better multicultural workers, improved international community relations, and an enhanced corporate image all over the world. But it's not just about hiring someone from another country; it's also about teaching employees how to conduct business effectively in that country. AT&T does this through educational sessions for expatriate workers in order to acclimate them to a new society and to minimize culture shock.

There are also global diversity organizations that bring AT&T's vision of international inclusion to reality. They go beyond just employee recruiting and customer marketing. The AT&T Procurement Organization is responsible for negotiating and contracting for goods and services for AT&T. Annually, it purchases over $15 billion worth of products globally. It also oversees delivering goods and services to international businesses and their customers to guarantee quality and value.

AT&T has recognized the inherent value of global social responsibility. By connecting with and improving the communities where it has a presence, it can improve its reputation and image through actions. AT&T Pioneers is the world's largest company-sponsored community volunteer organization. In 2006, the organization donated 14.3 million hours to community outreach activities. That's more than $257 million worth of time to better all involved. Nearly 365,000 AT&T employees and retirees have volunteered in six continents through the Pioneers.

By expanding in to the global marketplace, AT&T has greatly increased the imperative for inclusion within its naturally diverse environment. Through organizations, education, social responsibility, and integrated business strategies, this expansion has been highly successful for employees and customers. AT&T has truly blazed the trail for global diversity in a global company.

Case Study: IBM

Global Workforce Diversity is a cornerstone of IBM's strategy to differentiate itself as one of the world's great companies.

IBM's commitment to diversity is such that the company has initiated a global strategic framework for diversity to address how it responds to the plethora of emerging trends in the countries where it helps its clients do business. Overall, IBM's intention is to create an environment that maximizes our employees' productivity and connection to the enterprise on a global scale.

Achieving this goal requires IBM to use diversity as a means to engender the innovative culture that defines the company. That means extending beyond the traditional subjects of diversity—race, gender, genetics, religion, disability or sexual orientation—by aligning diversity with globalization so that it becomes a natural extension of the company's strategy.

IBM is especially sensitive to the accepted norms of behavior in the various countries where it operates because the company has a long history of doing business outside the United States, IBM has employees in more than 75 countries, and it does business in over 170 countries. Additionally, since 1975, over half of IBM's annual revenue has come from outside the U.S., while since 1993, more than half of its employees work outside this country.

Nearly 70 countries where IBMers work have diversity legislation in place. That's almost double what it was just three years ago. This is the new era of diversity, the global era. To operate successfully, IBM believes it must be especially mindful of how it respects and values differences among people in countries and regions.

Chapter 15

Research and Measurement

Contributor: Greg Morris,
Senior Consultant, Novations Group, Inc.

Diversity and inclusion initiatives are business initiatives that must be managed in the same way that an organization manages any other business initiative. Effective strategic business planning, executive sponsorship, communication, change management, project management, day-to-day execution, and measurement all are regarded as business fundamentals for most functional areas in an organization. They are givens when it comes to product development, supply-chain management, manufacturing, and so forth.

When it comes to diversity and inclusion, organizations often regard business fundamentals as optional. The reality is that most organizations are only beginning to apply rigorous discipline to their people programs, including their diversity and inclusion initiatives. This is especially true when it comes to measurement, and the void is compounded by the fact that many organizations are unsure of how to measure diversity and inclusion results.

An organization's ability to assess its current state and measure progress is a business basic. In order for senior leaders to fully champion diversity and inclusion, they must be able to view the diversity and inclusion imperative through the familiar lens of the business fundamentals.

In this chapter, we will explore the following questions:

• Why should organizations measure the impact of diversity and inclusion?

• Why isn't measurement standard operating procedure?

• What are the main priorities in measurement?

• How can organizations establish the business case for diversity and inclusion through measurement?

• What are some current trends, opportunities, and best practices in measurement?

The Measurement Journey

This chapter will explore what it takes for an organization to have a strong measurement component of its diversity and inclusion initiative. First, we look at the benefits—what's in it for the organization that gets diversity and inclusion measurement right. We then will narrow our focus to a set of logical diversity and inclusion measurement priorities. We examine why these measurement priorities are valuable primarily when they help demonstrate a return on diversity and inclusion investments. We will describe some cornerstone Best practices for measurement, and finally, we'll highlight some trends and opportunities. Along the way, we will begin to realize that every organization already has valuable starting-point data with which to start the measurement journey.

Benefits of Measurement: Why Measure?

Best-practice companies regularly measure the health of the organization with respect to well-articulated success criteria. They live the adage that what gets measured gets done. Indeed, measurement has value in several general situations:

- When an organization simply wants to do due diligence in prioritizing and managing its human capital initiatives before and/or after the fact to strengthen the business case and better define success, by objectively assessing the impact of initiatives or quantify the impact in order to secure program sponsorship, doing so in language that is more meaningful to sponsors.

- When an organization wants to understand the relative costs and benefits of a variety of interventions—e.g., instructor-led vs. online training, communications training vs. project management training, whether or not to conduct a needs assessment before a training initiative, etc.

- When an organization recognizes there are tangible costs of inaction. The costs of taking action often are very tangible (e.g., vendor training costs). The benefits of taking action can seem intangible or difficult to measure, but do need to be measured.

There are multiple ways that a robust capability in diversity measurement helps an organization to move forward:

- To identify business needs, priorities, and opportunities

- To determine how to address business priorities

- To establish clear performance goals for teams and individuals

- To evaluate progress versus plans

- To isolate issues requiring special attention

- To assess and foster organizational capacity to recruit diverse talent

- To assess and foster organizational capacity to achieve engagement through inclusive management practices

- To meet legal requirements

What an organization inevitably wants to determine is whether or not its diversity and inclusion efforts are effective and why. This raises the subject of maximizing the return on an organization's investment in (a) pursuing broad diversity in its workforce and (b) inclusively managing the organization so that everyone is engaged in the work at hand. We will look at return on investment (ROI) more closely later on.

Why Isn't Measurement a Standard Operating Procedure?

If the benefits of measurement are so numerous and compelling, why is it that so many companies struggle with diversity and inclusion measurement, or avoid the topic altogether unless it is a matter of legal compliance? The answer to this question seems to be that diversity and inclusion practitioners feel distinctly less competent in this area than in other less-quantitative aspects of their work. Measurement typically is not an area in which they have been trained, and there is no extensive body of work to support a diversity and inclusion measurement effort.

The discomfort is not surprising. After all, even the most senior corporate executives overseeing multiple functional areas receive scant measurement training unless they are in or from the Finance function. The discomfort felt by diversity and inclusion practitioners reflects a general reluctance to measure the impact of people initiatives, as well as sporadic implementation of metrics elsewhere in the business. This is compounded by the fact that many diversity and inclusion departments are skeleton crews that decide they cannot spare the resources to make measurement one of their standard operating procedures.

By demystifying the practice of measurement, we can begin to find that building or strengthening a measurement practice is an essential, attainable diversity and inclusion goal. We demystify the practice by exploring the basics—return on investment first, and then a handful of keys to the success of best-practice companies.

Measurement Priorities

Desired business outcomes must determine an organization's measurement priorities. In examining the connection between business priorities and diversity-related measurement priorities, it is best to start at the top, with the organization's overall strategic plan. A logical sequence of questions emerges:

- At the highest level, what is the organization seeking to accomplish?

- What are the critical success factors?

- How do diversity, inclusion, and engagement affect the success factors? What do diversity, inclusion, and engagement have to do with achieving the critical successes that will lead to the organization's overall success?

- What specifically will diversity, inclusion, and engagement success look like?

- Where does the organization stand with all of this currently? What is the current state? What is working or not working? Why? What data do we already have? What additional data do we need to collect?

- Given where the organization is currently, where does it need to go next? What behaviors must change? In other words, what now needs to happen with respect to diversity, inclusion, and engagement, so that the organization's overarching critical success factors are achieved?

- What actions must be taken to achieve the desired results? What are the tactics for moving from the current state to the desired future state?

- What data will tell us if the required changes are happening, including behavior changes? What data will tell us if the changes are having the intended impact?

Once an organization completes this self-examination, several topic areas typically become priorities for measurement:

1. **Inclusion, Engagement, Productivity** Assessing the general climate with respect to full inclusion of all employees in the life of the organization; assessing the emotional connection employees have to the organization, which influences their willingness to demonstrate consistently high levels of contribution and commitment; assessing employees' perceptions of diversity and inclusion; and assessing how all of this ties to productivity.

2. **Recruitment** Enabling recruiters and managers to develop and implement effective strategies for attracting and hiring a diverse workforce.

3. **Retention** Enabling managers and other leaders to evaluate specific strategies for retaining high performers.

4. **Development and Advancement** Assessing the effectiveness of learning and development efforts; determining which specific initiatives do the best job of effecting sustainable behavior change and building capability in areas that are aligned with the organization's long-term direction; ensuring that all employees have access to job assignments and advancement opportunities that require them to use the capabilities they develop. Measurement drives accountability; accountability drives behavior change.

5. **Market Impact** Determining how inclusive management practices impact sales, market share, or underlying cost structures. The impact of teamwork between Employee Resource Groups and Sales is one of the more prominent components of this.

6. Compliance Managing the organization to the standards established in Affirmative Action Plans, Equal Employment Opportunity guidelines, supplier diversity guidelines, etc.

There is overlap in these priorities, but these are six general buckets into which measurement efforts tend to fall. In a sense, though, measurement is always about understanding and maximizing ROI—empowering senior leaders with concrete evidence about how diversity and inclusion initiatives do and do not drive organizational performance and bottom-line financial results.

The Business Case: ROI

Return on investment (ROI) remains more art than science in many of even the most functional areas. Nowhere is this more true than when it comes to how organizations manage their people practices, including their strategies for pursuing diversity and managing it inclusively.

Nonetheless, best-practice companies increasingly look for ways to quantify the return on their talent development, making better use of quantitative and qualitative data they already have and being more intentional when they seek additional data. Diversity and inclusion functions that do an outstanding job of articulating and demonstrating ROI will have an edge. A complete approach for examining ROI includes the following steps:

- Methodically answering the "Measurement Priorities" questions listed above

- Quantifying what is most easily quantifiable (e.g., turnover costs)

- Raising senior leader awareness of other clear impacts that are more difficult to quantify; using benchmarks provided by external subject matter experts to gauge the magnitude of the bottom-line impact

- Acknowledging the difficulty of proving cause and effect for diversity and inclusion initiatives, while demonstrating strong correlation

- Evaluating diversity and inclusion efforts with the same ROI standards used elsewhere in the organization whenever possible; do not hold diversity and inclusion to a higher standard, recognizing that investments in other areas are regularly and comfortably approved without comprehensive ROI analysis

In their calculations of ROI, best-practice companies seek to measure a wide range of impacts:

- Market Impacts
  - › Sales

- › Customer satisfaction

- › Market share

- › Geographic reach

- › Reputational capital

- › Economies of scale/cost structure

- Workforce Impacts

  - › Recruitment

  - › Attrition/retention/turnover/replacement

  - › Unexcused absences

  - › Safety incidents

  - › Discretionary effort

  - › Innovation

In the final analysis, it is the market impacts that need to be central to the ROI analysis because these are the ultimate evidence of whether or not a company or organization is fulfilling its stated mission.

Best Practices in Measurement

The following is an overview of four measurement best practices for diversity and inclusion practitioners, some of which have been mentioned here already. This is not a comprehensive recipe for everything one needs to know or do about measurement; instead, these best practice provide a foundation that can keep measurement efforts on track and ensure that they support the organization's work as much as possible, even when other priorities or simple lack of experience stands in the way of a conscientious measurement effort.

Link Diversity and Inclusion Metrics to Business Outcomes

In 2009, Novations and Linkage revisited and duplicated their 1998 examination of how the field of diversity and inclusion is evolving. The 2009 study included scores of companies of all sizes and across many industries. By far, the principal measurement challenge most often cited was the need to link metrics to business outcomes. This is the core practice from which all else flows.

In particular, diversity and inclusion metrics must be driven by the organization's highest-level goals. In order to have real value, diversity and inclusion initiatives must deliver progress in ways that are aligned with the organization's overall success. High-level goals will relate to the market impacts listed earlier—sales, customer satisfaction, market share, and other impacts directly having to do with growing the business.

Workforce impacts are secondary, relevant because they lead to these market impacts. In general, recruitment measures, turnover measures, engagement measures, and so forth ultimately are important only if inclusively managing recruitment, representation, and/or engagement translates into better bottom-line performance for the organization as a whole, as defined by a documented strategic plan.

Ensuring that metrics are tied to business outcomes gives executive sponsors a reason to care deeply about diversity and inclusion success. It can bring clarity to a company's goals and desired outcomes, too. It's one thing to try to grow sales across the board 10% next year; it's another matter to realize that sales can grow by 10% overall only if the company figures out how to grow by 20%, 30%, or 40% in underserved markets.

The "Measurement Priorities" questions discussed earlier offer a straightforward, disciplined path for linking diversity and inclusion metrics to business outcomes. In examining these linkages, concepts such as the service-profit chain can help to illustrate how people results bring about business results. For example, the service-profit chain shows the chain of cause and effect that leads from employee engagement and internal issues to profitability, growth, and return on investment.

Leverage the Power of Engagement

Best-practice companies are aggressive and creative in measuring engagement:

- Senior executives, managers, and other leaders join the diversity and inclusion function in championing engagement measures as critical business measures. They view engagement as one of the major levers they can affect to achieve market impacts that grow the business. They know that executing the business plan boils down to engaging everyone to do their best work.

- In measuring engagement, they employ a wide lens. That is, they have a broad view of what can lead to engagement, and their metrics track representation in recruitment, retention, and advancement. However, they also tend to look at underlying determinants of engagement, which lead representation to be what it is. They measure the effectiveness of communication at all levels, performance management and feedback mechanisms, development support, the job assignment process, other business processes, and infrastructure.

- They carefully design quantitative engagement surveys to ask about obvious and non-obvious engagement factors, but they also make the connection between engagement and other indicators of organizational effectiveness—qualitative measures such as focus groups and interview results, 360 feedback, even simple process measures (e.g., Do 100% of employees have a development plan?).

- They methodically measure the relative importance to their organization of the various factors that bring about engagement, so that solutions are targeted accordingly. When necessary, they hire experts to analyze the data properly. The experts identify causation where possible or strong correlation between specific environmental factors and engagement, and they put the results in language that non-experts understand.

- They specifically measure employee engagement with respect to diversity and inclusion. Are employees at all levels responding to the business imperative out of a commitment to compliance, because they identify with leaders who are championing diversity and inclusion, or because they personally recognize the business imperative and have internalized it?

Insist on Accountability

In implementing their diversity and inclusion measurement practices, best-practice companies set themselves up for accountability:

- Whenever possible, they collect baseline and/or external benchmark data (e.g. best-in-class companies) before they begin a diversity and inclusion initiative. This gives them a standard for comparison. In some instances, they may be able to establish an internal control group as their basis for comparison.

- As early as possible, they spell out a vision for how to effectively present data—for example, taking the time up front to design a diversity scorecard where they have not had one previously (see "Trends & Opportunities").

- Whenever possible, they set expectations early about how measurement results will be used to hold employees accountable. In a timely manner, they build a user-friendly infrastructure that gives visibility to metrics and makes individual and team performance standards clear. They position measurement success as being inseparable from performance incentives such as individual compensation, an employee resource group's budget, or a marketing department's advertising budget.

- They integrate diversity and inclusion metrics with other key metrics, for example, by including key diversity scorecard measures on their management dashboard.

Best-practice companies also take action after they have measured and obtained data:

- They follow through in using the mechanisms described above.

- They conduct post-implementation surveys using the Kirkpatrick evaluation model, which evaluates four levels of learning (reaction, knowledge, behavior change, business impact).

- They use the data, actively supporting behavioral change and process improvements where they are needed, pursuing root-cause analysis until effective solutions are defined.

Embrace Measurement Basics

At best-practice companies, diversity and inclusion practitioners may or may not have extensive background in measurement. However, as a minimum, one or more champions will have enough awareness of and sensitivity to measurement basics to be able to make use of expert advice when the experts speak in language that non-experts can understand. Relying on the assistance of experts whenever necessary, they are able to draw sound measurement conclusions, make decisions that are supported by data, and avoid common measurement pitfalls.

In addition to the best practices already covered, here are some topics for which a little knowledge can go a long way:

- Assessment as the objective, measurement as the tool to support the objective, having a measurement component of any diversity and inclusion initiative—measurement (quantitative or qualitative) is simply an organization's tool for figuring out where it stands and where it needs to go

- Quantitative measurement instruments and understanding of when one tool or another is more effective

  › Surveys – climate, engagement, customer satisfaction, training effectiveness, communications effectiveness, philanthropic impact, reputational capital

  › Performance measurement systems

  › 360-degree feedback

- Qualitative measurement instruments and understanding of when one tool or another is more effective

  › Interviews

  › Focus groups

  › Direct observation

- Striking a balance between quantitative and qualitative tools

- Simple statistical measures (e.g., mean, median, standard deviation) – awareness, but not necessarily the ability to actually do the statistical analysis.

- Data interpretation

  › Root-cause analysis

  › Willingness to engage in discussion with experts about how to interpret data, including results based on statistical measures of moderate complexity

- Awareness of which measures are the most important measures in the eyes of senior leaders.

- Emphasis on results

> › Kirkpatrick scale

> › Measuring behavior change

> › Measuring sustained change

> › Process measures vs. results measures

It need not be a major undertaking to acquire this basic knowledge. Much of the statistical analysis undertaken in the business world is far closer to arithmetic in complexity than to calculus or even high-school algebra. Diversity and inclusion practitioners empower themselves tremendously by seeing measurement in this light and being willing to have the measurement conversation.

Move Beyond Representation

When looking at the numbers, best-practice companies are continuing to move further and further beyond representation goals originally based in compliance requirements. Of course, many companies began their diversity journeys with compliance because that is what was legally required and the business case for diversity had not been clarified. Compliance goals seldom are defined in terms that are closely aligned with an organization's highest-priority goals and measures. Naturally, representation goals have been achieved, but business results often have been disappointing nonetheless.

There has long been a revolving door for traditionally underrepresented groups at companies that pursued diversity in the absence of inclusive management practices. The revolving door still exists; ownership of retention and development goals remains ambiguous in many organizations. However, retention, development, engagement, and productivity goals are becoming more commonplace. Organizations are finding that it is by inclusively implementing the best management practices that substantive business goals are achieved.

Best Practices vs. Common Practice

These are best practices. They are not common practice. By patiently adopting these practices over time and deliberately moving to do it step by step, diversity and inclusion functions distinguish themselves internally and externally, commanding greater mindshare from senior leaders internally and, in terms of making an impact, moving ahead of the pack versus peers diversity and inclusion functions.

Trends and Opportunities

Related to the measurement best practices, several promising tactical trends have gained momentum in recent years and warrant greater attention. There also are some tactical opportunities that deserve special mention, including:

- **Partnering with product development, sales, and marketing** Perhaps evolving from fledgling efforts to look at ROI and increase the focus on overall business outcomes (Best Practice #1), companies are realizing now that a diverse workforce can indeed have a measurable impact on sales and profits. For example, more and more employee resource groups are being tapped to evaluate and propose new product ideas and new marketing campaigns. Companies are seeing results from these collaborations, especially consumer products and service sector companies. The collaborations are changing the vision of who the customer is, and also the process for finding out what the customer wants.

- **Diversity Scorecards** Organizations are establishing scorecards and other visible means of highlighting diversity and inclusion progress and opportunity. Some organizations have attempted to tie metrics to performance incentives, although diversity and inclusion measures typically remain a very small component of how performance is evaluated and compensation is determined.

- **Economic Climate** Companies that are maintaining or strengthening their diversity and inclusion efforts during the current economic downturn are doing so because they see this as a fertile time for diverse new ideas and new ways of attracting customers. In the present climate, such companies typically have incontrovertible measurement evidence to justify moving forward. Costs associated with undesirable turnover or other opportunity costs of not acting to promote inclusion are carrying the day. Where companies have not been able to document such evidence, almost invariably they are pulling back on their development of the talent pipeline, their succession planning, their budgets for employee resource groups, etc.

- **Broadening Diversity** Organizations define diversity more and more broadly. The measurement focus remains heavily on women and people of color. There has been worthwhile measurement focus on generational differences, and there has been some increased mindfulness of how diversity and inclusion are relevant topics for white males in the workplace, but many other forms of difference are under-examined (e.g. what it means to include and engage a working mother, someone who is differently abled, someone without the organization's traditional conflict-resolution style).

- **Return on Investment** There is increased discussion of how to measure ROI, but actually measuring ROI is still an elusive ideal for most organizations. They may measure turnover or engagement, but the measurement impact is greater when it is translated into an ROI, an estimate of shareholder valuation or some other traditional measure of financial impact.

Conclusion

In this chapter, we:

- Established the importance of measuring the impact of diversity and inclusion.

- Investigated ways to include measurement in standard operating procedure.

- Reviewed the main priorities in measurement.

- Discussed how organizations can establish the business case for diversity and inclusion through measurement.

- Analyzed current trends, opportunities, and best practices in measurement.

Every organization must move forward with measurement at its own pace. At the same time, it is very much within reach for organizations to apply measurement discipline to their diversity and inclusion work, to measure the business impact.

For some organizations, D&I measurement may start with one fundamental success measure for a single diversity and inclusion tactic—perhaps a training program, a mentoring program, or an employee resource group activity. Whenever the organization strengthens the link between its diversity and inclusion objectives and its overall business plan, progress is made.

Interested in learning more about how your company's D&I programs compare? Learn about Diversity Best Practices' new DBP Assessment & Benchmarking Tool at diversitybestpractices.com.